# THE MOUNTAINS OF MOURNE

by

Séamas Cain

(Photographs by Gloria DeFilipps Brush)

# THE MOUNTAINS OF MOURNE

by

Séamas Cain

(Photographs by Gloria DeFilipps Brush)

Oyster Moon Press

Berkeley, California

THE MOUNTAINS OF MOURNE
by Séamas Cain



ISBN: 978-0-578-21651-5

Additional copies of this book can be ordered from LuLu:
http://www.lulu.com

*Oyster Moon Press* is a non-profit, surrealist publishing co-op that
originated in Berkeley, California.

www.oystermoonpress.com

## DISRUPTION & REMEMBRANCE: A PREFACE

Yes indeed, I have been to the Mountains of Mourne in Northern Ireland many times. Benjamin Cain, my great-great-grandfather, lived in those mountains before fleeing to the Miramichi region of Maritime Canada. He was an Irish rebel. He was "**Wanted**" by the Law in four countries. Documents of the time reveal that he was once in the custody of the Sheriff of Northumberland County in New Brunswick. Escaping from the dank jail in Newcastle, he fled to the Gaspé peninsula of Québec, near the Percé Rock, where he lived for many years among people who were also hiding-out from the forces of the Law.

The Percé Rock is a huge rock formation on the tip of the Gaspé. It is a massive block of limestone that over the millennia has become a sheer natural arch in the water. One writer described it as "a monstrous giant, pierced through by an immense eye, now green, now grey, now blue or violet, according to the moods of the sea." The Percé Rock itself is in a state of constant erosion and disintegration, and parts of it show a tendency to collapse. It is an entirely natural image characterized by impermanence, a slow-motion crumbling, and a singular beauty. From a distance it is possible to hear the sounds of a great multiplicity of particles and pebbles rolling and dropping downward into the water or the sand.

André Breton visited the Gaspé during October of 1944 (the year I was born). He recorded impressions of the Percé Rock in his book ARCANUM 17, "a hymn of hope, renewal, and resurrection." He reminded his readers that "nature renews herself and that death is only transitory." He called the Percé Rock "a razor blade rising out of the water, an image very imperious and commanding, a marvelous iceberg of a moon stone."

Late in life, Benjamin Cain returned to Northern Ireland, and to the very parish where he had been born. People said he had come back from the "wild wastes" of Québec. Benjamin went on long walks through the Mountains of Mourne. Those mountains were his *eidolon* for some permanence in an impermanent world, a random world.

I still have relatives living in the Mountains of Mourne, who have survived more than one civil war. For these relatives, though, the Mountains of Mourne were "just but a resting place of birds."

Séamas Cain
Warrenpoint, County Down,
Northern Ireland

## HISTORIES

a ploughman arose like wings of swans
on a cold weir, a lottery of mildew
the ploughman gasped at a sunken field
i trampled up & down with blows
i measured the rubbage on a beetle
while day's air atomized my forest
the ploughman discarded a broken tool

a lace-maker flung herself from a tower
high noon & noon to night gave a silver
portrait of the knuckles of this jumper
but when at withering of the tower
an adolescent boy gnawed
the filaments of a virgin
swords grew out of the
impudence of a causeway

punctures of the commandments
lunged at my smooth wet throat
i decorated the stench of the weir but
smote the changes of a great philosophy
the amputating swells of philosophy
roaring in the leafless
top of a crystal forest

crockery filled up the churchyard
revelry swung in a sad mutilation
of vowels in a granary; i expired
passing to a mournful atheist
whirl of the entrails of a swan

along the sea's side, as though
the dizziness of necromancy
grew there far on the sea's waste
nothing but vaseline was
scribbled on a mackerel
the vapor vapor chased
shipwrecks pierced through
the crust of a gentle sea
frail sea, fed with a green light
the source of water ringlet anatomy
shipwrecks pierced the metal sea
water leaves, immovable & bright
this vaseline cheated all shrubbery

dawn slowly turned, in passionate
magpies, daintily colored
first white, now burned

## A SCOTTISH CASTLE

whitethorn shall rise again through
the air, greatly polluted air
leaning up from a gem-studded trunk
penis, & hoaxes of penis
with a sob for wax & the weak
you & i saw a red-shank bird
you had heard the wren & the grouse

beetroot & kelp destroyed all snails
i fell on the mud, horses
syphon of toothache the fumes
three hundred grouse fell on me
in the empty waltzes of cheese
a creeping old wren, full of sleep
crept to walls of cardigan or fish

sacred boys carry a fetid talisman
walking over a path of stones & profanity
until they settle down to the
shock of analytical thought

& yet, how the crazy boys of the sand
crystallize like a sack of old vegetables
where for swing of a sorry place
all the rough metal deteriorates
yes, what place have you destroyed?

talisman, but a compound blasphemy
i wrapped my face in my hair today
whitethorn struck at gorged actors
stars were larger than berries
every tooth in manure of a wren on
the broad floors of a scottish castle

ashtree or phlegm & reeds
a sacred boy is lonely & longing
the grouse if a contour to watch
the heart in me leaps like a
whitethorn shall not break
i turn & urinate to the west

a fumbler sits on mad boys in pain
i see where the fat actors lie sleeping
delightful whitethorn delightful grouse
& the mingling of the grouse there
at the foot of a mountain

i disentangle a braiding
of whitethorn & talisman
children bear it with staggering
the old wren is very quiet

## INTRIGUE

the dead white rivers pour out
naked & gleaming bodies exactly
corks are detached from salamanders
that break the very notion of arrows
& axes in your spilt wine, sour wine
a pair of pliers is heard despite
a cold landscape in whose hollow
a trombone blanches the dew

palmistry conducts a throng of gadgets
you & i are startled on a couch of rushes
listen! a suction of linen on a desk
a girl can make a comely universe
out of corks & knitting-needles
a universe of huge white creatures

i examine wreckage behind a human rosette
the tops of the dogs are feathered
i watch curves that shake the
plumes of the yellow grasses
a cormorant pokes at a jar of mutton
long breathing comes from our bodies

an eclipse bubbled beneath us
as we pursued a tatter of thighs
i arose in a hard ghost the
intrigue of the dragonflies
an assessor betrayed the public treasury
as white horses went sinking away & away
to convict the yellow bubbles of thighs

a horn sounded beneath a flatterer
a sailor drowned slowly as
drift from the quadrants
wrapped around a serpent
hands & faces were creased on hazel
the hands were sinking into a canal
those faces were chirping
those faces were blotted
above the matted jowls

i threw bottles at nothing but wisps
cumbrous mules gave a whinny & hiss
precociously the mules to speculate
down from the hoofs of ancestors
a clatter to the slopes &
towels to muffle the clatter
monstrous starlight under
the shadow of a demon

## PERISCOPES

i recollect the odors of
the sound in the stars as
an oarsman memorizes grease
ah! when will you turn to the world
of lightnings, in oaken murkiness
the murkiness of oaken lightnings
i walked by a woods of distant odors
a kerchief of sturgeons
rustled behind thorn-bushes
old murmurous droppings
old murmurs of sturgeons

my mistress walls up my odors in sound
no weasels live there in the bushes
artery goes to the sling of tittle
over the reverie of all things
my mistress is unhappy with porridge
no weasels live there on the heights
my mistress puts bricks around a statue
she breaks a flask by the
plains of the sea's edge
wails of the monocles of stars
forgetful of the green of grasses
as though the double of landward reverie
as though the double of landward sound

put out the periscopes of the "3"!
throw soft sour berries over the
tops of the periscopes as a
windowsill purges the millions of "3"
yes! if only you had wept
for the explosion of a shoe
dandruff of the words on a starling
the starling brushes pebbles
against a rough haymouse for
smells of the wiliness of a mob

& when will you turn to the
enamel of atheists or potash
the atheists look from the sheen
of earth at a distant sheen
squint of the rattles of a nut-cracker
like a small withered leaf in the
broken wheeze of periscopes

starlings shall mingle no more to empty
ribbons & berries over the haymouse
brakes on the irrigation of ribbons
that destroy the farthest periscopes
where only the imperialists would dare
to speak of the masochism of a turkey-hen
less soft than my breath

BLACKBIRD

i observe a twinkle of
the nucleon of murder like
metal riveted fast against
the uranium of a coracle
or the white snowdrops
floating above the coracle
the snowdrops drift in
the gates of my heart

i found a bird's gut within
the odor of new-mown hay
a virgin of wild friction
fell down like berries
a weapon can give bread in
the sound of a shore far away

stubbornly * * *
the snowdrops * * *
nor knew i * * *
embosomed apart * * *
the snowdrops * * *

i limp amongst the shore-weeds & brown
i examine the veiling of a rabbit-warren
my weight is crushing the sand & the shells
insects & birds fidget in
the crevices of the shore-weeds
dried raspberries sink through
a chant of love on my lips

see! golden debris is singing
where all will be barren & gray
the antistrophe of a horseshoe
moving over the dripping trees
i gesture with a priceless chafer as
though the blackbirds would hasten away
clouds have become nothing but
lumber for blackbirds who try to
escape from the moan of the seas

look! golden debris is grunting at a
blackbird whose flaming ran to the edge
of a cloud, turning & turning to go
i learn the usages of the snap of a
piccolo far from the hazel & oak
an artist makes a hissing woodcut
high as my saddle bow the
blackbirds moan at the sea

i reject the wandering & milky smoke
that covers the whittles of a faun
winds flee out of a vast copse

TOMORROW

a slithery fish drinks from me
avalanches drink from the fish
this fish under a golden cyclone of light

i fashion a stronghold out of hay ricks as
the barbarians move among the fountains
pigeons will settle on armchairs
to watch the barbarians fidget
i summon an ironer of the pigeons

the woods' old night
drowns a hard lighthouse
like shadows on the tinted colors
of the Mountains of Mourne
those incredible reaches
ever hand in hand
antiquaries build a nourishing crust
as they sit on a pale strand
the chattering intruder explodes
& closes like an obscure star

birches collided with sexual freedom
above each hooked knee
calibrations & plummets of birds & fish
languished with a dreamy gaze

i shake, like a frighted bird
clear your throttles for a whip
of the white gown of a poltroon
lawns of clover will become
the inflammation of tomorrow

i bridled a horse in water
the squalor of a grapefruit
i knew the drama was over
i grabbed at a plate of citrus fruit
planetary lime, stimulus of lime
i heard machines as my eyes grew dim
candlesticks were changed into machines
with all the ancient sorrow of a
boat of pencils, thirsty pencils

i sigh & moan, like a colored findrinny
dreams ride out again in
the whine of a cuckoo
i monitor my heartache & temperature as
the findrinny examines wounds on a cypress
cycles of reverberating sound
move over a dull purple sea

RAZORS

i wallow in dirty water that
in unmortal silence ignites
a yellow carp the smotherer
of its own melting hues
a heart & a cistern shake
as the carp leaps over the
ambers & blues to uranium
nevertheless nevertheless
i wallow in carp water

i want a rat's landscape
soft light in shallowing deeps
the processes of cannibals
or a christ-fisher

breezes came from land
then, in a trance, a cascade
of feathery quires as the
seasurges of uranium & gorse
blew from a dying flame

or, was it the stillness of
fishspawn that glazed in the
smouldering fires & rocky ashes?

a tumescent horse raced towards me
sadly, i haltered my bruised horse

the sun's rim sank, but
it left breath to trees
yells arrayed their rank on rank as
mere packets for milk-clots & huffs
i crushed a fading crimson ball

mouse-holes are lapping
the floor of a mouse's hall
the neon of gunpowder & razors
more level than the sea
or vomit the melting-point
of loving phantasy for
a corrosive seagull

moon like a white rose shines as
neon for thatchers of detergent

low murmurs rode on the
lava of geraniums to gallop
where many shells of
twisted trumpets collapse

## THE PARASOL

a sob of wax pushes a
weak mutilated saddle by
fractions of my watercourse
you have heard of the rest
the bizarre isthmus bizarre offal
a white horse went away like a
drop of water running down
a lamp-shade drained away
i fell on the path of a gang
of vaporous wrestlers
they were holding seashells

creeping ducks, full
of sleep, with boys!
clear ducks, pour a
twinkling into a bladder!
yes! how ducks showed me the
weight & motion of a sand-sack
crystal veins & slicing veins
where for swing of the vapor
of muscles the wrestlers in a
locomotion of freckles i expire

what place have you taken?
plunder of sedge in a sequence
of plunders! you too are
old with your memories

the naked wrestlers were following
my ducks with many broad gestures
a frieze of the ducks breathed
nothing but a purple holy terror
munitions lined the floors of the
godly capitalists; a mash of the
contractors of water shivered &
turned to a longing pony the
pony was encased in salt &
covered by a gigantic parasol
the pony was hoping to leap like
an insect into splatters of water

barbers on a hill turned over & over
the barbers moved westward on & on
jumping to a song's yellow milligram
the barbers followed the salty pony
& hesitated, where the pony lay down
sleeping until starlight was erased

the stripling of a thunderbolt
imploded at the foot of a mountain
beeswax chilled every virtue
with staggering & sweating, but
millstones tumbled down from
the gem-studded wrestlers

## THE HORSE'S BITE

breadcrumbs fell, &
the world grew dim
splinters of breadcrumbs
mounted & a woman bound me
my long belly & her unknown belly
as breadcrumbs & shouts were like
triumphing metal around me

the world grew dim
to herself enwound me
i am dull & backward
like a pinecone, or a
cloudy globe of spittle
a horse had felt weight
but not my expectations
the horse's bite & tin eyelids
you neighed three times

i saw dandruff on a teapot
women raised their lamenting hands
ragwort & pumice as you rustle
& modulate with many a grief
the sweetbread of a grenade
out from the anti-human lands

you & the women roll merrily
but knowing tumult & strife
the larches were heated & scorched
merry as dogs or birds to invade
the magnesium of camel or tillage
when women dance
to a fitful measure
rosebud to be reborn
like the speed of herds of salmon
wafer of the ferret of slavering

horses & birds will obey your whim
i counted up the birds but i
refused to count the larches
you shall know the adverbial leisure
horn & horn this martingale
or the cold moist alabaster

gently it grows late
your tresses are frozen as
love & sleep await the
spume of the lines of crayfish
where would you be when
the white moon climbs?

## EXTINCTION

wolves fashion me out of a wild thought
my wild thought & my fashioning, as a
redwing tips the plaid of the maples
there's no man may look at the wolves
& covet the ransom of crayfish or
the strings of a crayfish
the wolves revolt, as when
newly grown to unravel the
marble of ventilation

a she-wolf pulled down a pale deer
at the station of riddles of hooves
at the hour of a moth's
brilliant snarling
yes yes a snarling
this she-wolf is kinder yet for
swamp-rushes as a pestle for starshine
she could not weep that the old are
destroyed in the studs of downpour
the folly of being at the
weld of a roaring or mill-pond
predation that is ever kind
predation upon a throne of wolves

tomatoes form an outer mosaic
from which i am hanging paper flowers
in the wind the padlock of rheumatism
because i am alone, & wolfishly nimble
i hear a tainting of wind
i am wolfishly translucent
murmur of a dimple of the wind
warp of a ghostly boat & clouds
i am contented, for the
places of whispers & wolves
the travels of laughing
& eating with wolves
cracklings of the piracy
of a tin-whistle among
pigeons & bees, while the
she-wolf closes against a gray
witness the racket of a
cricket who but awaits the
hour the wolves will vanish
a quiver over the twisting of a wasp

i remember the beauty of wolves
wolves in an uprising

## FEATHERS

nuns & i speak to dead worms
loosely along the dim ground
avoid or escape from the billowing
sails of a thorned journalist
with many more bells than Murrisk
engulf ourselves in the waters of
a silver corridor of bracelets

owls are ruffling & huffing
step by step down into an abyss
emphatically shade your eyes
from the mortise of forgetting
no & no, nowhere in any shouts
wedges of sails, sails of mist

by demons flung in the cool air
i examined a silhouette of feathers
to the salt eye of ferns
quivers under quivers you conspired
faded when the seas distilled
nothing but a handcuff of convections
a bear was groaning
bear, far sung

devils were cloven
as crippled devils
warless, grown whiter
than semen or mushrooms
i caressed a young devil
who had stars for brains
i pulled back from a drizzle
of the terrible black enamels
i wanted to go from dew-cumbered
devils with their memories
of face-powder & rough skin
one halibut was placed
on a bier of lichens

chickadees builded their nests
a darkling of a fish of curds
that once more huffed & puffed
the aerations of eyes or a lichen
of the snowflake of singing

fresh glue comes up my muzzle
as the owls grumble & collapse
now in a wide place of shadows

i am lying on my back near a swamp
you are sitting on my belly your
knees in the soft mud around me
the yolk of wanderers & liars
the reins by my side

QUALMS

alphabets showed the journeys of slaves
in an antique winter, burning winter
i moved out the artillery of a graveyard the
disc of the graveyard sparkling above me
where feet touched writings like a small river
gardeners worked on parcels of consolation
my left foot gleamed like a
momentary phosphorus flame
on a water-hen of reverie
under the deepest shadow of the
fractions of vituperation

i found a ring hung on a wall
streamers of turnips, conformistic gardeners
with a flare in the rings on my fingers
i ignored the phantom of a purple seed

i made sparks about me in the air the torches
mists had gone deep into the artillery-shells
under a doorway, out of sight
lava flapped & flapped on a mutineer
that dead mutineer held a second light

i hang a star there amongst the shouts & hail
a rook that is sifted out of fireworks
shall never mount so far
rice of eclipse & rice of oscillation
the rook & the hail are nearly hidden
unloose a swab of lightnings in
a stall of tormented dolphins
the hailstones are prevented from soaring
i could have thrown down that star

violent swabs gave earthly delights
i released a swab of lightnings in
the spite of tortured dolphins
meat of the symmetry of instruments
symmetry of the meat of instruments
i sat down & stabled with cumbered pigs
tubs of supplement of a hedge
i sought the part of dolphins as
though bitter hours were nothing but
the collapse of an embankment or
the sinking of a piratical smack

slime was not distant from my door
indeed, but my sky-high qualms were distant
time on time made a pig slippery
redwing, i said, & the insects fell & scattered
while down through prints of scales & sea-born
crustaceans i began to disintegrate

## THE LADY O'HANDRAHAUN

Yearningly / longingly / to the
Sweating of the brain * thorns as
Thorns reaching~ lovingly
She was like a pale rose
Thrusting / attaining / thorn shrub
She was tenacious cause of irritation
Short sharp pointing hard leafless
Varying stem

Rose of red
Rose of white
Luxuriousness / beautiful / yet
Simple affection~ lush
I trust you (she said)
Plant with prickly stems
Growing with becomingness
Abounding and good vigour
Ornamentation~
I love the radiance of true
Simplicity (she said)
Speak (I said)

Eyes the color of russet
Blue white skin of tissue
She was purity of parchment
Prepared as a surface :
Interwoven mesh~
Mottled by bleeding injuries on
Occasional rareties /
Mark of archaic hurt and
Scarcity~ lack of densities
She was volume of the
Crowd~ objectified~ obsidian
I am the whirlwind (she said)
Alabaster face (I said)
Many streaming panting wind
And rain to the hard and
Glassy dark rocks /
High to the suffering shores

Cargoes of the land
Cargoes of the wood
Spouting to sound by blowing
O the Lady O'Handrahaun
Driven (she said)
Bursting explosion~ blowing motion
She was holding her own face
Cold fingers : to graze past something
A light touch in passing
Loveliness / lovely
Brushing finger motion
Royal face thunder~ continuously
I in brightness and with luck (she said)

## CRAZY JANE AND CRAZY MARY

"Motion
That repeats
Itself in circle :
It seemed an easy game
To change the form /
Transfiguration
It seemed an easy game —
To change what was given to me
Into nothingness / nothingness
It seemed an easy game —
To change
Into indefinite
Laziness each definite passion."

And that is what Crazy Mary said!
To be sure, that is what she said!

"Motion
That repeats
Itself in circle : sweat /
Pulsation — the sweat of
Struggle in life!
Motion
That repeats
Itself in circle : illusion /
Tiny mirror motions —
You were always the same!
Motion
That repeats
Itself in circle :
Without affection — you gave
Penetrating subtle insult."

And that is what Crazy Jane said!
To be sure, that is what she said!

"Now : at that void
I have finally collected
Each of my
Contemptuous sensuous expectations
Now : at that void
I experience
Sheer nothingness the longing
Motions/ event~ totality~ motions
Now : at that void
I experience new
Emotion — that gives glimmerings
It is the only one you recognize
It is the one that only you recognize
Illuminations : in a struggle for life."

And that is what Crazy Mary said!
To be sure, that is what she said!

## CRAZY MARY SCOLDS THE IRISH REPUBLICAN ARMY

HOPE : burning slowly
In a raw fire
The tough log burning
Among grey rocks

Gesture remains : it
Measures the void
CEREMONY sounds the
Limitations of affection
Rituals : unknown
That express themselves and
Nothing else
You may endure
But : I am lasting
Passion to one final irrepeatable
Beat of brain and blood

TRAGEDY endures only in ashes
Persistence is merely extinction
You have been commodified!
Slow-burning hope has at last
Consumed itself

Remember remember :

Keep the powder in your brain
WHEN : every motion has been
Extinguished
Sounds grow intolerable
Then : I, Crazy Mary, will
Descend — shimmering, shadowy
On a prow
Piercing the wild
Waters

Remember remember : Tragedy
Is only a memory

## THE EXHUMATION OF MOZART

and sycamores shall
have no tablet
the dead tackle naked tangles
shall be tar
with the swan in
the swig and
the west tortoise
when the whistles are
picked tincture (vaccine tinge)
and the uranium
urine gone
valves shall have
sweetbread at towels
and wind-vanes
though vermin vertex
go vinegar vertebra
shall be vellum
though tendons sink through
the varnish vaseline
shall rise again
though hawk's talon be
lost a test-tube
tether shall not
and velvet venom shall
have no velvet venison

and towers shall
have no uproar
under the taunt of
the swimmer and swirl
vowel vomit lying voltage
shall not utensils windily
twist on tanners
and talkers when
symmetry gives way
strapped to a texture yet
turnips shall not break

and tide-mark shall
have no thistles
no more may thaw cry
at the toadstools
though timbrel tin be
walnut waltz vibration
and virus as vitriol
and waterfall waterfall
the warble rabbit-warren
wart hammer through toothache
break in the
tattler till the
verdure breaks down
and velvet wasp shall have
no velvet water-cress
and velvet venom shall
have no velvet venison

## DON QUIJOTE

Muchos pocos hacen un mucho,
la cereza, el cobre, la cereza,
la cereza, cereza, el cobre.

Salir atestando, el búho,
el perejil, el cobre, el
cobre, la cereza, cereza.

Cuando la puerta es baja,
hay que agacharse ~ la anémona,
melocotones, los melocotones.

Hay un juicio, los melocotones,
cono de pino, ortiga, la noche,
noche, cono de pino, la noche.
Tiempo tras tiempo viene, la
servilleta, la mañana, la mimosa,
mimosa, la servilleta, la mimosa.

Zurrar la pavana, pececillo,
urraca, mármol, mármol y loto,
loto, y loto, urraca y mármol.
Llorar con ambos ojos, lagarto,
limón, mariquita, mandíbula,
mariquita, lagarto, mariquita.

Lo mas encomendado lleva el gato,
hiedra, serpiente, iris, serpiente.
Palabras y plumas el viento las lleva,
petróleo, agua, agua, herradura, agua.

La calentura declina, espina,
roble, casco, casco, halcón,
ganso, espina, roble y casco.
Dijo el escarabajo:
"Gusano de resplandor,
cubre de escarcha, paredes."

No morderse los labios, niebla,
vellón, red, niebla, abeto, red,
abeto, labios, niebla y niebla.
Mondar los huesos, haces
de leña, armiño, olmo,
olmo, alce, olmo, olmo.

Suceda lo que sucediere,
dragón, pan, polvo, pan,
polvo, pan, polvo, pan.
Salir de lagunas y entrar
en mojadas, cenizas, delfín,
cornejo, y cornejo.

ELEGIES

Thus is sighing ice of
year ice heighing waltz, I
roll up my thigh skin, brittle
to the anger searough woman
the statue vomits over
stone in stone we
are in stone truthstunted and
verbmissing in stone
their mud and their mouths.

Ice invokes the waterstone
clamped in mud turned spigot in
mud the mouth
wordswollen and swallowed.
And this night man who is not submissive.
My ears have now vanished.
My mouth tasted his quiet.

Tomb is unforgiven to blueness,
over the far foreignness (I
have forgotten) with this
sigh signing Black bed end.
The lightloose thimble favor
of a friend, the ghost in
triple-tiered Busting.
I scratch the front clover thistle,
violet against the green yellow.

We are,
without the red edge of dawn
cool breath,
this branch gathered man.
We spat and we whimpered,
withoutpart and gushloosened,
bewimpled,
eyelids tremble.
We broke the woodmaster's awl.
We are shut, late,
white sheen within shimmerwhite,
we glower the moist dawn I
am under his (eyes) curse
within curse.

QUESTIONING

Does a basket know the gourd where
the lemon dwarf explodes, and
the golden rattlesnakes glow in the
dark harvest wart, where a gentle
photograph blows from the blue
melody, where the bell's jade stands
quiet and coming-of-age towers up?
Does history know a hobo's nutrient?
Traintracks are where, oh, airwaves
are where, hunters would like to
go with a circle's vomit,
oh my pygmy gateway!

Does a sorceress know the source?
Its quilt rests on a poison, the edge
gleams, the rags glitter (mold chitters) and
marble wands and gardens stand, a horsefly
looks at smoke images. "Poor lust! what
has uranium done to blood?" she said.
Does a skin know warm bushes, honeycombs,
staghorns, and star vines?
Wavechange is where, oh,
watermarking is where
the grass would like to
go with fishnets, oh my dome dream!

Does birdsound know
the mountain cerebellum
and daydreams' cloudy
weeds? The trail seeks
raindrop's hole there in
the fiber's niche; the
ancient shifting of water dwells in
bridges and peaks; the
pattern's icicle foliage falls
sheer and the mushroom over it.
Does a gem know the sword's doorway?
Rockpile is there, oh, glacial-scar is
where our moving island leads, oh,
fibers, humming, harbor, let watermarks go!

## THE RUSSET MOTH

To rest on the surface of a fluid.
Weeds and water web the wrack the shore grass.
War is finished.
I am severed, woman, not white,
the pearl, the pearl touching his hair.
She is a moth, and russet moth,
the moon milk white war wings
of moth, and russet the sunlight
the commotion over the body.
Menelaus, a moth touches the hair of Helen.
She verbs me, and
verbs the moth, the
verb foam light.
The moth is not pale.
My skin is not white.
Sun dries the lemon.
Clay crumbling in the blood.
She slips into the sea, the
cumbersome weight of sea,
the lemon sea, and weeds of war
and wrack web the water war.
We rest at the shore, the
clouds, the eyelids, and the
surface of a moth, the fluid,
the belly at grass's end, the
pearl, the burnt moth,
the severed moth.
Helen, look, the sunset mist wall,
the desolate, and Queen of Egypt,
the desolate, the color of brass, the
striations, and sunset mist the wall,
the folded up, the cropped, the
coiled, the twined about.
All eyes lift in a mime.
Helen lifts the one eye of mine.
She lifts eyes with eye-powers, and compulsion.
Shadows trample the rhythm of horses, horses,
horses, the horses, horses, the oxen, the horses,
the black oxen, all the black oxen.
Menelaus, listen, the war ox, the black ox,
the war ox passes, in narrow tide, the
dripping, the suffocating in water.
The war ox is not vain.
Spirit breathes in momentum, in history.

## THE SHATTERING OF AN ORCHID

Menelaus and Helen move to
mountain shadow, moon winter
with wolf is white, the vain black
ox, the killing, and every eagle face
of Egypt, in mountains.
We endure the cloaking hunger,
and bird cry, and moon harsh
murmurs the murmurs of Menelaus.
Helen is pulse is beat, is heavy, the
heaviness, and the clamor of Menelaus
clinched up to that beat of pulse.
He sits on white rock, the whispering,
the ward wind narrow of rock, the
rock whispering, the dripping.
Egypt and Helen creep close,
grey and yellow eyelids.
Tongues are wet, and running wetness.
He grips the mouth of Helen,
the hoarse mouth, the wind
mutter low in the throat, the
wailing, the deafen'd Helen.
Sun goads the waters.
God sighs.
All experience is overthrown.
All existence will collapse in bottomless space.
I plead for the end of creation.
Menelaus, the gods, the
shattering of the orchid,
above the orchid.
Menelaus, the gods, the
shattering of the orchid,
the gods, above the
orchid, the shattering.
Menelaus is elemental
is the moves in music,
above the orchid.
Menelaus moves in music,
elemental, the orchid.
Sky waste is his stomach.
Menelaus mixed up all the parts
of Helen in one wild withering.
Self is darkness. I am darkness.
Passion, the mere images on
water, and world weight weave
and war bend in water.

## THE COVERINGPOOL SHADOWS

Helen, listen, the shadows wait,
and shadows wait amongst the
trees, in the trees, the bruised,
the pitched up, the inserted,
the trees hold up the sky.
Passion is images in water.
Egypt and Helen disconnect the
limbs of a dull golden statue.
Morning bird white is morning is bird is white.
Helen, unloose the thong, and world mirror.
Helen goads the war water-sun,
the sunwater, in war.
Mirror and earth are overthrown.
Egypt is overthrown.
Disassemble and reassemble the parts
of Helen, but in new juxtaposition.
Music is not dream.
Death is moving in the fluids of Menelaus.
Menelaus, look at moonrise.
She cries out like a cow.
Menelaus, look at moonrise, the
fluids, the moving, the moonrise.
The Queen of Egypt, in troublous crush, the
curving, the worn curving, the apple wood
falling, the apple wood torn away, the carving,
worn carving, and the Queen of Egypt is all
troublous crush'd against the wood, the
war wood, the apple wood dropping.
Helen is foam is flames.
Roots winding round Helen, the
brambles, the knotted brambles.
I enfold brambles and foam flame.
I enwrap selfness and berries
and coveringpool shadows.
Water sleeps.
Sun, between darkness, then sun, the
brooding the rapture, and water sleeps.
Queen of Egypt, look at sunset, the whirling
rose, the whirl of sunset, the roseflower, the
rose of war, the war wood rose, and set of sun,
the whirl, and sun white hair the gleaming wet rose.
Come close to me.
Moon is drowned.
Moon is drowning.

## BLADES BRONZE GONG BREAK BEAT

Helen is entangled among pale sand, white
and red sand, the foam wandering, the sand,
carving the skin, the sand, the wandering, the
dream of foam and fire, the white and red sand.
Menelaus, to his dragging long hair.
Menelaus is deep and shadowless.
She loosens the casting net, in casting
net, in Helen, the wind wrong, the folds,
the cloud, the net, the loosening Helen,
shadowless, to the net the Helen.
Not fire not pale.
Fire is pale.
Weight sky blades to the lonely the hold.
Menelaus, blades bronze gong break beat to
wheels, the wheels, wheels to Helen, to the
deep, too deep, the war wheels, the long hair
dragging in the sea-fish net, the
war sea net, casting net.
Heart beat quick, to Menelaus.
Heart beat quick, the break beat, the
bronze heart, the blades of heart, bladed
heart, to Helen, to the Queen of Egypt, in
quick gong, the beat of Menelaus, the beat of
blood, the beat of wheels, the beat of wheels.
Weight sky blades, the bronze blades,
blades of sky, to Helen, the sky, the
break of gong, the break, the break
of sky, the pulse break, break beat.
Wheels, wheels, the long
hair dragging in the war
wheels, death hair.
Menelaus, Menelaus, the silver
hands amid the water, the waiting,
the image in water, amidst the water.
The Queen of Egypt hid, to
the secret, the bitterness.
He raves at hazel wood tombs.
He is dim and raving.
He sinks down under the
water, the awaiting, to await,
the gleaming, amid the water,
under the water, the silver hands.
He is gleaming as he sinks down under
the water, amidst the water, the bitterness,
to the secret, the water-reeds round him,
the dimness, the silver hands, the tomb,
the war war reeds, the hazel wood.

NEGATION

Twilight, river reaches. He raises his arms.
The Queen of Egypt, without
beauty without terror, to plunge,
to starve, to overwhelm, and twilight,
Menelaus, twilight, and Menelaus, the
reach of river, the negation, the negation
of all immeasureable waters, to starve.
Twilight, river reaches.
Menelaus and Helen, the negation,
to plunge, and twilight, twilight.
Foam light wide, hazel great
roots compassing stones and
briars, the negation of Menelaus,
the division of Egypt, in briars.
To overwhelm, and twilight,
the briars, the reach of river,
the Helen, the circle the root,
and foam the negation of history.
Menelaus and Helen, the negation, to
overwhelm, the stones, the compassing
circle, a width of light, dull light, the hazel,
the roots of hazel, the war roots, the briar.
The Queen of Egypt, in grey trees, the low
wood, the war wood, the land wood, cover.
Moisture and wonder on the
tongue, the briar tongue.
Amid white hovering animals
and wings, Egypt and Helen
vanished in breath, drowsy breath.
Sorrows, the loud marsh mud bird, the
loud lowness, the sweetness, the power
sound of drums, and mud breath, drowsy
breath, the tapping of mud marsh wings.
Sorrows, sorrows, the white animal,
the moisture, the shining, the war
head, the vanished voice, the wonder,
the briar, the war briar, the foam, the
sudden rustling, the marsh, the mud,
the tongue, the hovering tongue, the
width, the sleep, the smell, the Helen,
and the sorrows, sorrows, the marsh
mud, the loud lowness, the fierce bird.
Menelaus, I seek dilutedness,
the extinction of creation.
He is as though reflected in empty water.
Twilight, river reaches.
Sorrow's marsh mud bird is loud.

## RAINFALL

They gather round her.
They gather round her, to the Queen of Egypt.
Rainfall fills the leaves, wets the apple blossom.
Rainfall, rainfall fills, the matted leaves, the
leap, the weapons, the paleness, the wetness.
Rainfall, rainfall fills, the matted leaves,
the matted blossom, and Menelaus,
the matted blossom, the skin.
Rainfall, rainfall fills, fills the leaves,
the matted leaves and matted
Menelaus, joyfulness, the waters,
the war waters, the loins.
Rainfall, rainfall fills, fills the
blossom, pleasure, the wet
leaves, to the Queen of
Egypt, wets the Queen
of Egypt, leap of Egypt.
Rainfall, rainfall fills, and Helen, the matted leaves,
and rainfall, the rainfall skin, and rainfall, and Helen,
and rainfall, and wet blossom, and rainfall, rainfall.
Menelaus, your mouth is but my
mouth, your brain is but my brain,
your eyes are but my eyes, the
regret, the terrible sweetness.
Rainfall, rainfall fills, the matted leaves, the
leap, the weapons, the paleness, the wetness.
Rainfall, rainfall fills, the matted leaves,
the matted blossom, and Menelaus,
the matted blossom, the skin.
The Queen of Egypt, predatory,
and white drops, leap on the waters.
The Queen of Egypt, matted
skin and hair, predatory, and
white drops, and a fruit.

## STARS

They are whispering together.
Menelaus dances in a starry dance.
Mysteries are bitter and silken.
Menelaus moves the
dance, the terrible
sweetness, the
whispering dance.
All the constellations dance round
Menelaus, mysterious, silken, bitter.
All the predatory constellations,
chaotic, dizzy, dance round Menelaus,
destruction, the stars dance.
All the stars dance the destruction of universe.
All the constellations, the stars, the fruit,
the stars, the silken stars, the mysteries,
the stars, the whispering stars, dance
round Menelaus, the bitter dance.
I am dizzy.
A constellation moves the
dance, dizzy destruction,
and a terrible sweetness.
All the constellations dance
round Menelaus, and mysteries
move the dance, fruit moves
the dance, the starry dance.
All the stars dance the destruction of universe.
Menelaus, starry Menelaus, silken Menelaus, the
dance, the dance, the whispering constellations.
Menelaus, your silvery skin is wet.
Encircle him, rushes in the
waters, the swamp rushes,
reed-rushes, the war rushes.
Encircle him, the constellations, the war
constellations, the skin, the skin stars.
Encircle him, the silver, the
fruit, the mucus, all the mucus.
Mucus rushes like the waters.
Encircle him, the constellations, the war
constellations, the skin, the skin stars.

## FISH FLASH THROUGH THE WEEDS

Menelaus, in delusion,
watching the shrubbery,
between the leaves, yes yes,
between the moment leaves,
leaves in moment, the sunlight
fall over apple wood.
Helen, the flash, flash, the flash,
and bone shadow, weed shadow,
the fruit weed, fish, fish.
The Queen of Egypt, in delusion,
between the leaves, not watching,
between the leaves, dusty leaves,
burnt shrubbery, between the leaves,
the momentary leaves, the sun breaks
wood, and the sun breaks applewood.
Fish flash through the weeds. Fish flash
through the weeds' edge, and edge of wind.
White form of Queen of Egypt, mist broken,
voice through the whiteness, voice through
mist, voice through, and broken form.
White form of Menelaus, the broken, the
whiteness, the voice, the mist form.
Moon is shining moisture on
the rose, a light bright rose.
Sun is shining moisture.
Sun is moisture
on the rose, the
shining, the sun.
Moon is a rose.
Body forgets the spirit when the body loves.
Queen of Egypt, sing away his memory.
Fish flash through the weeds.
Here is shadowy line.
And a sunlight fall over apple wood.
Fish flash through
the weeds' edge,
and edge of wind.

## THE REVOLVING ISLAND

Menelaus, red surge of the
waters, birds like dreams, and
wandering land, revolving land.
Menelaus, the revolving island,
and red waters, and redness, the
wanderer, the birds in surge.
The Queen of Egypt, wind forgotten, the
surge, the safety, the dreams, the redness,
and redness of morning, and moaning of
Menelaus, waters are silent, the sun, the
drying pool, the sun pool, dry sun.
Helen, lily, the lily of the foam,
the sun pool, red pool, red foam.
Helen, lily, the lily of the foam,
the creeping, the keep, the
cold, the red birds, silent birds,
dry birds, red dreams.
Helen, lily, the lily of foam,
redness of foam, foam lily,
the sun, forgotten sun,
and red sun, the moaning,
the redness, the wind.
Farewell well, farewell star, I fragrant you.
Birds were silent. We saw the birds.
It is war's end wars end,
Menelaus, the surge, the
sun pool, the purple, the
fruit, the vapor, the hair.
Helen, lily, the lily in
foam, lily out of foam,
lily of foam, red foam,
foam lily, the sun, sun.
It is war's end wars end,
Menelaus, the color, the
vapor, vaporous color, war's
end wars end, and Queen of
Egypt, and Helen, and morning,
purple morning, purple fruit.
Farewell well, farewell star, I fragrant you.
Menelaus, red surge
of waters, birds like
dreams, and wandering
land, revolving land.
Menelaus, the revolving island,
and red waters, and redness, the
wanderer, the birds in surge.

## :: CUTS INTAGLIOS ::

out from perils of the sea
a scottish centaur pushes
in the dry earth loam
diaphora, variance
polyp & octopus
over the red wire
& over the berries
counterpoints, with
old carved stones
:::::::
the centaur heard a sea-surge
for the centaur is submarine
yes yes, "submarine," & the
centaur fights a martlet
under the pepper
under the wire
under the olives
under the berries
by cypress, & mares
the slanted mirages
assimilated mirages
mirages as ruining
the old social order
:::::::
the sand that night
like an otter's back
(submerse the maritimes)
here & there an arm
or a leg upward in
the cold night with
trout, submerged
by the eels, the centaur
under my sphinxes with
sham egyptian columns
& murmurs as flutes
on the river the cold
reeds of invisible river
:::::::
osmosis, ideogram
black walnut, almond
(submerse the maritimes)
a mist weighs down
the wild thyme as the
scottish centaur destroys the
cuts of an imprint of intaglios
)))))))

# LULLABY

i fell asleep upon a lonely
honey-pale murderess
a yellow murderess
she dwelt in a cabin
warm cabin durable cabin
no boughs have withered because of
the daggers that are stuck in them
the murderess herself has withered
the cabin will perish, disintegrate
because of her, in drifts of cod &
the yellow tufts of a heckler

i know the leafy paths that
consume a lard of the
whims of a vile ghost
who comes with a crown
the sound of the fiddlers
becomes a kind of gunpowder to
explode my clandestine smile out
of the knell of a splenetic fiddle
i know where a dim moon
robs the sour ghost of all existence

the murderess & i wind & unwind a
burn of cascades of music
on the island lawns
or on the tower lawns
the sacred tower
if deaf & dumb the abscess
to turn a booty the dragonflies
that made this music

the murderess knows the
smirch of turpentine
for she gave all her
maze of sputum to transform
my femurs in the withering of
the quicksand on the mantelpiece
she cried when the moon was
hiccups & sweetbread

let a peewit call to the
sturgeons with its detergent howl
the murderess longs for
the merry & tender
rock-fish that haunts the
roots of lilies in a swamp
for the roads are unending
rainbows admit nothing but creaks

the honey-pale murderess lay low on my bed

## SUNDOWN

one-hundred chimes had ceased
though i stood as a lingerer
before the starch of chimes
i hoped to follow trapezes over mad granite
surges of light would bear me upon a stair

my skin grew sore at the touch of beechwood
plummet of the acid of seaweed in hard acid
opposed how i stood by white-haired children
a brown wheedler on a brown peninsula
while a woodpecker destroyed
a berry in a coffer
of frozen reticence
woodpeckers came & leaped in the grass
racer as a spoon for desperate effigy
sadly, men barked of a name
that held a desperate horse

a caterpillar of jazzdance
passed over a lone mountain
& the starch of all the vultures
while a monotone drifted out of the gray

i measured the circumference of fetlocks
a wide stair dropped on foam & penitence
i meandered along the fringe of sabotage
hair was whispering in my purple slime
rill of pebbles against
a foal alone in spite
that foal will be so dull & unsubduable

my shoulder-blade, that opposed a beehive of fish
fell more to a battle of long chimes than granite
i mumbled behind a sorrel & a tree
sundown threw me in the surge
i am crawling in twists & wrinkles
until bees emerge from a flit
of haddock at an apron
i see an old healed shape to lie upon

i masticate at the very sound of a stonechat
feast without dreams or fears
the mere stratagem of sinking frogs
an endless war without languor or fatigue

## THE SHIVAREE

brides never turn their eyes
a fawn spits out the ellipse of a
violin that fades & flickers & dies
tinkles unfold on a prow of wafers
as a kiss on dim shores away away
i put a fork on watchers of a globe
with music of the sighing spray

i turned down the volume on a radio
fuchsia, in very white streaks
when, like a brown bee

i crossed a drunken misty sea
famine reddened a window before me
i touched a hundred muscles in white arms
then i criss-crossed the edge
of an ancient white beach
i was intoxicated not intoxicated
a staghorn / not ferns & sand
the staghorn / weeds & eggshells
before the fall of teardrops
i did not know if a turret fell

away, like whirling flames
the tinkles of powdered flames
brides & runners stabbed me

away, like drunken flames
the ellipse of poison & flames
a sneeze protruded from a gnarl
brides fled by mist-covered sand without
the deep bleeding that ruptured a tornado
the deer & hound without
mitres of poison or sunbeams
no more on the phantoms of
rivers the onions or paper
swaying a bright head the
depths of exertion in eggshells
flags were streaming in the clear air

you speak of fire & a manly bright body
powdered alder, vitrified alder
before an old line begins the
geologic line of old music
passengers descend from outmoded transport
they are demented & somewhat violent
they grumble & squeal & cough
brides & runners stab me
in exultant fire old fire

courtly screws, on brides
with rings of pagan gold

WAR

the soldiers are dead & stony in
a deep horror of eyes & of wings
an adze chops up all the vertebrae
the touch of the butcher
is gently received
boys shall listen
& rise up & weep

i cover myself in a yellow mantle
the armies are stretched like
bowstrings or a sanctified
waterfall of disfigurement
the boys enter & wash
themselves in the waterfall
they sweep as shouting & mocking

battle * the detritus at the
bottom of a dank pool
battle * a gateway of brass the
spinach or hunt of pinlights
the boys enter a strongly armed tower
the tower is covered by a sheen
of buttermilk, & mistletoe

oxen move over young weeds
the growl of the sponges of radium
& of old wounds, & sleep
i drink a strange juice
to the octave of war
the limbs of the soldiers are toasted

you & i pursue an old man
surrounded with leaves & dreams
jade of the fireworks of a plumtree
the plumtree clings to burning stones
i inject a narcotic into a soldier
a weathercock flaps in the hot wind
wires on the burning
jade of wide plumtrees
you & i destroy the
cooing of a musical
stallion the smile
on a taoist face
rose-beds of musical destruction

the soldiers will rise, making
clouds with their breath
the soldiers will see
an ivory cormorant
the clay underneath them shall pant
chess-games of meteorites will be
trampled beneath them in death

LIZARD

i remember the bitter sound
of the oceanic piccolo
i remember the white centuries
of quantities of paper the
lichen the same as the moan
paper is made out of ashwood
as linkage for the throbs of clay
springwater touches a burning anvil
while heated bicycles touch my throat
the white-eyed oxen are lowing
undulating the kinks out of a poplar

mild lichens drive the dust with paper
woe of clay the yellow temperature as
landsmen or seamen move round a luster
of aches, & oscillator of aches
branches roared with
yellow planetary paper
love-making moved as
the lichen pierced its own
ledge of the premium at odds
a tall boy slunk in a great jar

lichens are born of starlight & kittens
starlight comes from the hardness of paper
tendon of the skyline to conspire
i laid the sorrels at
the roots of pewter &
kittens were weighted down by paper
a lizard & a tiny bird lay by me
i saw the grasses as white as pearls
a delicious flash for the mutilated bird
& the lizard was gone in the distance

an elegy from a hot limitless wire
moved over me, binding me down to
the harvest of constellations of lizards
white croziers of the many
veinslashers poked & exposed
my horror & my sneakiness withal
i dripped my cold blood in
the centuries of a thick
charter that burst into flames

i watched a falcon on the
wire for symptoms of a louse
hammers pounded out the names of demons

## NEEDLEWORK

i create a soft whine
of fireworks to love you in the old
mediation the mediation of a speed-boat
but it had all seemed like
mere twigs penetrating a skull
insects are roving over me
i am as weary hearted as that
surgeon with a marker
of stripped tendon

the old brown thorn trees break
in the ammonia of touchdowns & rattles
under a bitter black wind that
destroys the sodium of muddy spearmint
my courage breaks like an old
skinburn the burn of swimmingholes
but i have hidden in the fall &
yelp of a dirty parachute of milk
the wind has bundled up the parachute
by the musical staves of a peat-bog &
thrown the thunder on me
thunder itself invites
me to the future

yet now it seems an idle
situation closing the
weal my utmost weal
a fat boy sat motionless
grown quiet at the draw
of tenement in whitethorn
he saw the last sparks of
tiredness that orbited skin-pores
in the trembling blue-green
pillions of a gash of needlework
a moon, worn as if it
bundled a marsh-hen
washed by spearmint's waters as
bullocks cross over a
sieve of the marshland
washed about the stars & broke in
the pillows of insects of sweetness

but i had a thought for no one's
scrounger but the scrounger
that makes me beautiful

## THE MIRROR & THE CHEMIST

oh destroying animals! sink
deep down into a thin ventilation!
my wailings grow distant
oh flames on these burning animals!
your wailings grow distant
nominator the pigeon pigeon
where ever is a sundial
the brindled fish are playing
for no live otters live there
talons of the sunbeams
push through a crust of reverie

the empty sweetness alone
a brindled fish over the verdure
spirits come to a gnarl of
mucus that suckles a zigzag
a pigeon sleeps on her nest
mulberry above the naked chatter
not lost in star-fires the
skylarks & ghosts or fly-paper

mosquitoes & a zigzag
flutter down to earth
those pigeons shall
stretch, curious to
see what a saddle of water
tries to capsize & swallow
over the tops of the tide

abrasions prevail on a chemist
a motion of branches is naught but
a mirror beyond the sea the stallion
if only your shoe was a paper of
woodbine to comb my long yellow hair

pigeons will come no more to my side
fish eat something like mince
despite the painful bright sunlight
three pigeons turn to
the rest of the flock
i admire the finality of birds
a tree makes a moan
hopelessness & beauty
are strapped to a quill
autumn, for beast unto beast

## THE DAFFODILS

a mallard blew at its chaperones
as if all foxes were not on the earth
pure brush & concrete
the end of change & birth
the mallard circles &
undulates as a lofty serpent
heaven & hell would die
the rattles of dimple & squints
in some gloomy barrow

do you disgrace me?
whipped over the locomotives
but where are your kith?
broken over the locomotives
into what landscape do you ride?
"my name is my land where tide"!

vermin & a crackle of distillery
drown sun & moon & star against
the smoothness of melted paraffin
vermin came with you that you came
no steeples for the tartar of puzzles

your feet are wet with foam
thews & stiletto in kerosene
from where the birds wing in
the vibration of a sunburst

you revolve,
with oysters tender & sweet
paraffin of oysters
weary of war

mist inhaled 27 ferrets, but
the ferrets are not more sad than
your burning secrets timid secrets
concealed before a peaceful monument
the lather of daffodils by photons
larger than any granary mouse

a lantern-holder made a strophe
in his own leafy forest
the drill of skin or vinegar
within thc waving fields of fern
a ragged ferret should be glad

peat-moss has gone into
a pencilled urn
a wasp is touched
by flaming chromium
on the terrorists lying slain

dawn split up a dark plain
a plain covered by ravens

## GRUMBLERS

my tragedy straightens a dragon
binding me down to
necklaces of wasps
croziers are forgotten
tragedy stands out against a dragon
when the fallen on fallen roll

a dark fly closed on the
weeds of a heron's velvet
what dried hammers made scarlet in
the crescents of freezing rainfall
the rainfall out of ozier & hide
to lull all snowflakes

a burning spot on my head
celery & jungles of charcoal
sadly at the end of tide
to escape a ruby that slants
driving the dust with force

talkers behind innocent men
dropping in faint streams
a caterpillar moves on a stone
a boy's marrow like flame
i pour a chaste kerosene on eggshells
earth more than of earth

i was startled by the howl
of the philosophers who fell as
once when thyme attracted magnetic
specks to a fiendish clerical chant
language, or cowslip in wickerwork

i avoided eyes the muslin eyes
eyes like sea-covered stones
pincers on a turnstile erased
all the memories of the whole
the delta of a radiant map
filled me full to the bone

i laid low the sorrels in mirth
foxglove beyond marmalade
the torches of mushrooms & shells
red & brown in the midst of
grumblers who grew quite fat
years, years after years

SLEEP

i was not weak i was not weak, in
the midst of venison & scutch-grass
a drunken anthropologist
pushed me to the ground
pushed me with contempt
he grunted & farted
so i watched when a
starling, like the starling that
reversed, exploded in silver & gold
when the sturgeons made foray
youthful reflections of merriment

i awoke: the strange horse
a warp of the silver of finger-prints
thrusting my nose to a
puzzle of fish of moons
that once more moved over
a ribbon of brood-hens

beautiful anthropologists grew white
beautiful anthropologists grew black
i said that i would leave the
stake the muffler for them

sturgeons had written with
their own oils & skin-scales
helpless, i lifted the drizzle
thin asterisks of drizzle
by soft red drapery which
pours down on a brood-hen
sewed with a needle
of a golden shift

so i lived & did not live, on
the surface of a kaleidoscope
in a long iron sleep the
drizzle of lemons & scrolls
at times my slumber disturbed me
in the rind of the icebergs
languorous noises of icebergs
when brushed with a dormouse that
sundered the eels from their prey

half wakening, a glow-worm was lifted
like a ciborium into harsh cold air

## THE APOCALYPSE

quicklime streams from the guitar
profoundly as it would never stop
guru of chop, chop quicklime
the hem of a pale dress
floats on a mint-sauce of thistles
i told a dressmaker to bring us to the
cypress of a cry within the sinews
dreams, from sun to sun
yonder the cataleptic violet
dream of the end of days
thud of sodium, lisps
of all sodium

christ is to wane
& the world be done
a certain tincture
led us by long & difficult ways
chop of the flames
drops of violets fall in myriads
shipwrecks are kept within
tangled creepers every hour

i am trimmed with a crimson feather
vexations of ice & of erosion
when people saw the cloak i wore
a kettledrum of horseflies washes
my body with a mire of the
distant oars of earthquakes
i fingered the kettledrum &
gazed on the sycamores of rye-bread,
like murmurs of the sea

herons are caught by thistles
dribble of herons
with a swift distress
the nylon of ancient cobblers
expectorant from herons
i bid them away & hold the
moors to a hard cantering
i heard a woman's voice run
like an exhaling balloon
every man knelt
before the unicorns

every man knelt

## THE PERIPHYSEON

The dividing out of all universe —
yes that dividing has withered because of my
sunburn intermingled with the sauce of a rifle.
A philosopher and I sat together at one cress,
listening to the oration of a maw, and that
beautiful mild snarl that became the lubricant
for murders, but a non-geometric line will
take us to sage as the musk of a gremlin
becomes the mast of the gremlin yet, if it
does not seem raspy, the udders of broken
vehicles will also sound raspy and metallic.
They are hard, very hard, and unflinching.
Our stitching and unstitching of a fish
does not satisfy the camels of my mind,
but it would be better to go down upon
your seething zigzag and scrub a fish's
pavement with all the severity of dung,
like an old pauper, in all the scrub of
obliterated fish. No boughs have fallen
or slipped because of lungs resembling
colored sugar. Those boughs have turned
and shattered cases and cases of the dray
of trumpets. Do you know of a sleepy
country where the radius of loiterers is
like canvas coupled with golden chains,
and mastication breathes fur and ladders
within us? A chess-king and a chess-queen
are traveling there, the horned or unhorned
interlude has made them so happy that the
people on the balcony laugh and the chimney
shakes with no wisdom, until the chess-queen
and the chess-king travel to find the overcoats
of an anchorite. Do you know, that the curlew
is happy and hopeless in the showers of a
woodcock? No, no curlews have withered
because of the dividing out of the universe.
)))))))

## THE FADING MEMORY OF HESIOD

Do you mask the least bit of yourself before me in the starry nights? Nevertheless, there would be only one thing that all masks and lands have entered in volts and sorghum together, the membranes of dirty strands that we must labor to banner with sulphur and maize to days following days for the memory of Hesiod. It's certain there's no axe at the day that is not fine for the repetitious passes of the utterly pale navigators, into all the kennels, since the fall of Hesiod, we but need a sad clear fishline to the solidified body of a dead dog. There have been lovers who tried to run up to that incandescent summit of bald mountain within the circumference of the death of Hesiod, so much compounded out of a dark scrag or the other scrags that ended hard in the night that they would sigh and quote the distant clots of a soft love-wail from the old poet himself, precedents out of beautiful bits.

:::::::

Which breaks in a poem do you dislike? You talked of poetry as if it might be nothing but one vertebra of a pine-tree in the tomb of a girl, for to articulate sweet hexes to the nitrate of the skin is to work hard or harder than the solder of dirt can be heard by a Benedictine nun!

:::::::

Do you want to be thought an idler by the nun, a quarrel of whirring with but one rein on the whirling? Do you hear the quarrel of humid bankers and schoolmasters as a delirium on the sidewalk? The feeble martyrs will call for the welder of splinters of a tongue, or the tongue that murmured with the girl's young voice, when bits of snaps that collided with streams of rainwater would collapse. There's many a poet shall find out the deceptions of the merchant's tongue, as this mythologist Hesiod did, a tongue to beat at in finding that it is ever young. But tell me, did you mask the least of yourself before me?

)))))))

## THE SPIDERS WITH MORGANA

An abandoned window-sill digests a wet pendant of
burns but more clearly a sequel of the checker pier
the pier when all the wild summer was nothing but
furls of ribbons and the thatchers lay down before
me. My heart! My heart! if she'd but speak to the
brindled fish you'd know the folly of the brilliant
cove of pains. Morgana and I thought to run to
the maimed old man when the wolves were afire
with clamps that awakened my old memories for
the periwinkles in a very hungry duel to survive.
:::::::
Though, your strength, in the duel, that is so very
much like the whitewash of an eagle, turn it, turn,
and twist it hard, spurt, it might call up a new and
far more passionate act then you or the very tepid
periwinkles that were imagined oh! My changeling,
I would be intact. Yes, I would be so utterly intact.
:::::::
Your well-beloved hair has crinkled like the points
of drawing-pins in the erosion of a virus. Little
shadows, no the little shadows, come, and come,
about the red submarine orchard in a scourge of
time, but time can but make slithery the flaming
enzymes in the crack of time. Though now it will
be hard, very hard oh! until I may smell the odors
of the electronic petrel bird, and so be patient, be
patient as the fish fin that will be aggravated before
spiders. But heart, my heart, there is no trample in
the trampling ornaments within my heart. Thus this
Morgana can but make me over to a hooter that will
bay at the kettledrums, because of that great animal,
and animal plunders, round and around her. I see
the gold fire that stirs about the encircled campfire.
)))))))

## THE FAIRY THAT SIFTED GOLD OVER A SNOWDROP

I threw offal to passionate boys, if a spray of octaves to a site was not certain, and they never gobbled up the espionage they found on all of the wreathes of the fairies. One fairy dropped his wreath, that it fades out from the incline of bile of the starlings, for everything that's clang to the rapiers on my maggot, but a brief dreamy measurement of rivets on the sly dead in a graveyard. Ah, never give the wails of the tortoise to zero, for they, for all smooth twilights dissolving toward a stake in a very dry field, have given their substance up to a closed settlement, and who could play it in the theater? I was exhausted by the morbid all-trembling archaeology that was but half yours, beyond cool nights with the mortises of a violinist, through the long years of the rims of the terminus of mud, all, and more than it all, would explode like the woodwork under the missiles of sleet, that dear words meant the end of heavy spores and heavy sperm and equally heavy insects for when we have blamed the gold sifted over a snowdrop. Or, if there needs be more, we saw the watercourse of a sunrise that would be harsh in and for the meteors of this rowan-tree on the hill that never gives all its texture to the clouds in its fading sky. However, for a rowan-tree, never give the wails of the tortoise, it will hardly seem worth it now!

BLOOD AND PARAFFIN

The stars, and the dark space, are better than the deep,
for terrible human fear to conceal itself in the darkness
like prowling snares and rotten figs. The astronomers,
and mathematicians, on the earth laid, shall listen to a
splintered teal or the disintegration of the parsley thus
before them as I will hear the shake and the quiver of
blackthorns in an orange summer. Then I would be so
loud, with a very occasional murmur, as my shouting
may become the snares of "being" for the woodflakes
in the night air. Then I will want to tear out the fires,
and the flaming stones, and batter the milky parrots
on a shaped tripod in most ancient conventionalities.
::::::
None says "no" when there enters this structure an
unfortunate herbalist, a burnt herbalist, as a broom
does not clean he convokes a mosquito forever flat,
making converse of wars and the bananas of a relic
(so the Syrians march on and march without refuge).
::::::
Are there sparrows, and so glass sparrows, that smell
the quadrangles of smells, where the foot-sole burns
on the stones of a ferret that walks slowly on session?
::::::
"This is a sorry place," I said. "This will always be a
quite sorry place." Blood and paraffin are dripped
or then sprinkled on the flower-beds. The Syrians,
for selves, whip those beds with wires on the pure
digestion of the old fumes of my shouts. Blessed
scientists move far off, and crush the hissing and
the hissing mashes of the last of the prairies, as
between a gateway of brass or the valves of the
nitrate in a snowdrop. One of the older Syrians
put a staff in my hands, and, then and there, we
heard a dim thunder, like a thunder of owls, or
the thunder that roused owls of old. Then all
of the red flashing smells were tracked, for they
went to the very red clay under the dim gray clay
underneath the robotic scarecrow skyscrapers.
)))))))

FREDERICK BARBAROSA

Cries will go to the absorption of vogue in a total writhing of turpentine, a writhing in a house of the skinners as puff-balls or grapefruit. Limbs of the corpses were thrown at a pile of old women, beside ink smears on rubbers of a mustard-plant in Frederick Barbarosa's hands. "Have you heard the birds a' singing in the night?" he said. "I solder in womankind the old panthers but the panthers make faint thunders, and the whiter courtyards on top of the universal panthers will hum (hum) in the lime tree. Writhe your taper of the vigor of your hand with signals!" he said. Limbs of the corpses were thrown at the rot of the soft Emperor, the old Barbarosa, who was listening (not listening) to the unavailing outcries from the loud old women.

:::::::

When suddenly, a field itself spurted the humble but very soft insipid spurts of lithographs that empty the heart on a red cape of old thunder. "Then Barbarosa will be uprooted," the women chanted, "he will be, he will be totally uprooted; eighty sea-gulls, shining in the colder sky, will soar down onto the masters of Hell, who could not run fast enough to out-run the running of several mussel-beds or olive-trees! So they will wear out the rock, to pray for an end of this flying misrule of gargle cake for the demon love of a boy and a godless mermaid at the monosyllable waterfalls that were shaken with coughing and broken by music from the daisies and a tweezers." "This though," Barbarosa said, "is nothing but a show for children, alone, in cages of macaroni and snow! I would spend purple hours as a beggar's painter in a marsh of tennis balls crushed by a rock, as a wolf chews on a martingale to sing ballads in chancel, so I may look on the blessed mermaid and no man will injure a sparrow, among the injuries of a sparrow, down the chain of small stones, to tell when I shall expire! Writhe your signals up!"

## THE OLD PIKED FISH

I touched an aluminum rhinoceros as it fattened the winds of the morning. Tinges of the imprecise light fattened a jack of all trades while a water wall fell on the creases of his forehead. The ribs of buzzards in this light were half lost in the sound of the mincer of heath, for the youthful sound, the thin youthful sound of a great grass-barnacle, or the nickel-plated beetle that cracks the very strong hoofs crushing the shining rhinoceros before me. I would see octagons of commas notched across the sea as the dawn flits, like a marble pitchfork in translucent marble air, sea under sea while I put my head on my knees. I saw a tidal wave of tide-mark ribs of stubble, as the silver demi-god's head is cut from his body. I will pour or splatter fly-paper and bricks as I make my way from the all burning surges of the white-red marble dawn.

:::::::

I knelt on the ground to pick up a stray board; then all the young men around me were longing for a rest from the incessant lips of a poplar-tree or the other lips, the chromium lips, that make the sands on the sea's edge glisten, and glisten so darkly before me oh!

:::::::

Then I will touch the nostrils of a sheaf of leopards as an old artist and the rhinoceros marked the "names" of hazel and oak. Is there style for a dimple, over as over, over and over, away on the surges, where, high as the melting-point of the seafarers, there was a sign with milky smoke that fled around me? Will I tremble under the skillet of pipers and the resin of surgeons, with the foam-flakes underneath me, locomotives as momentum of force for the old piked fish? My artist could not know the bird in secret in the dried orchard.

:::::::

Therefore my artist would do nothing but throw some revolvers that will freeze a cloth on my body like the metallic clasps on the dead songster birds. Then all the young men around me will be keening in awe of the lifting of the leanness of the birds and newts.

)))))))

## THE CORSAIRE, STUMBLING, AT LANDS' END

I was broken by the sea chases of pirates (after the hard look of a young man rejected me) with a brief skewer of cardboard eyes to hunt wolves in the night, for a scroll of the ripples of bowels; I slept by daytime, though voices cried, of the twitching in liver as bubbles. A number of men stood hushed on the pathway, as tails of the pillager of thrones, in folds round his eyes and (soft) his mouth, where rafters held out stump of the sad islands when for the islands were gone. I saw sheens of the shouts of coracles or eyes that glimmer like horses, when a dragon came out of that pudding on the table the murmurs were wrapped in my face and in my hair. A broken pirate touched the murdered spikes, larger than berries or white clouds. He still rises before me in my mind to see upon all hands, covered with dry scales and patches, of the reefs that lament the issues of the guardless churches, or the love of the looking-glass lettuce, bell under the Mountains of Mourne, or to assail the exhilarating sycamore. "Feeble," I answered, "I am so feeble, as pirates are stooping with snowdrops to the tinkle of a spotted doe, I will plough the faces a' shining with oddment and spool of the shake of wild spectres and a roe, while this place and that place, tamp the bodies, as tamp the wrenches of corn or the wrenches of the crumpled fuselage, in patience with the throw of the straw-death. Water, push down, and further down, in a dry turf-bank of scorn from my mouth, when I allow my whetstones of scorn to crumble in your mouth! A mob of pirates went by us, so huge or so intact, to prepare for sea chase. I will be forgotten then, in the tamp of the corn, transformed, transfigured, or lost."

## THE TRUE SOURCE OF CREATION

Will there be a final weather-vane for the <u>final</u> weather
on planet earth? Will I be green on a grass leaf during
this final weather? My Antinoös and I lifted our eyelids
and brushed on the grass the bugle of a slouch of verve
as we gazed at the woman at the heels of the bishops,
so much cooing that a windmill trembled and growled
for a weakling and a eunuch in the midst of a meadow
of nightmares, nightmares that were so written in red
ink, like the daydreams that were written in yellow and
red, that we could not ignore them. I like them, yes my
Antinoös, the dreams, my dreams, that forgathered with
my special releases, beneath the fangs of a vertex of curls.
:::::::
When will the eunuch make forays at the morning of day,
the forays at a glazed famine of oratory? Will I summon
a strange horse without any twist of girling or that other
twist, the twist of simple witchcraft? My Antinoös and I
knew shoulders and noses to thrust to flags, flags of red
and green, flags of white and green, that so moved in the
bottom of an ancient pit. Would we cook a traitor for the
ward of spittle in the <u>final</u> weather, or cook the dewdrops
that will be inspected for the true source of creation in an
odd time? A red car is brought forward on a sunken forest
with drizzle in a pouch revealing the cooing of silver webs.
:::::::
Will my Antinoös and I lift the lids of a dark and weary day?
May we boil a lizard with a manuscript, in soft red cloth of
turf, his bare toes or my silencer, in difficult sweat? We will
be sewed together with a smile of the sting of a plaice or a
softer sting from the marsh-hen. My Antinoös and I will
be wrought and wrought not, with his golden hair that is
illuminated against a polluted spire, as a fish in the water
goes hissing against a palisade of malaria. My Antinoös
and I will sleep as if our very lives depend on a total sleep,
though our slumber will be lightened when the sounds or
the odors of a metallic swamp can be heard in the rustle
and the torment of the claws and wings of the fetid owls.
)))))))

## THE IKONS OF THE BUTCHER

Tell me of the talk and the starlight in the muse of the belly of a wicket in crater that my friend slides under a worthy questioner a revelation of marmalade as cobweb under a butcher. Make me talk and talk, of this starlight, in my muse of affections! Dull butchers, no, all the dull men, held me half open at the astral windowsill of snails, no answer in answer moved slowly into a sculptor of tiny minnows, or very thick minnows, with branches of ferns that swayed in my fingers. Tell me tell me now, was this the pattern within the crater? Or, was there a cobweb in this crater? My friend of but yesterday climbs out of the wet veneration of sediment that pierced the snow-flakes in a liquid softer than mosques in terminal warm motion.

:::::::

But then I noticed the weariness of that music that waved in the wrap of a turf rick, the gnaws and snorts of the men who rooted around under that very rick. Meanwhile all my friends were gone, all gone, as they filled up the moil of the witch in a slit. "Sorrow," the butcher said, "is the whole of my memory." Pace the war, pace it, by a wide piece of wet plywood, or the plywood of a humbled and ruptured canal!

:::::::

But then I swayed my spittle on a branch of bells, while my eyebrows varnished a plateau in my mind, a plateau of ideas and ikons of dreams and release. The butchers, merrily, laid hands on my spittle, as the tab of shores of a golden orchard became the spittle of my rescue in time. However, waves of the spittle of the orchard blew, and blew again, a trombone out of the snatches of harvest, as backbone intertwined with backbone with monstrous intent. Monstrous sleepers, unable to sound the metallic wares over the trowels of shadows, were overcome by their anguish. They heaved the lips of a fold of a perch and the lips of the perch that the perch forced thorns to understand. Shake me yes shake me out of this mournful thatch of this time, as your waist becomes slender, more and more slender, in my astral time. What are the wonders, or a wonder, a marvel, for today? Indeed, what are my wonders?

)))))))

## ARCHITECTURE OF THE JUXTAPOSED ISLAND

I felt a terrible balm from the deluges of a tropical night with bells out of soft shine the branches of palms in my wet hands.

:::::::

The inlets of the Isle revolved and settled around the fruit of pomegranates and melons. Owls ruffled and purred, turning and turning out of whirlwind, or in the dry bundle of a young man's muscles, as I hoped I would foil and replace a basket at the calm pond. Sleepers, though, were stuffing and filling the thick bodies that were against them, to throw into maceration before the balm of night. Those moist sleepers were thronged to the traces of the wreck of a terrible conjunction, sidled on the glamour of a luminous tablet before a waverer. Salt was known by the beauty of adolescent faces, or the stature I saw in an adolescent baboon, faded when the passion of the vows of the spindle of tightropes faded. Sleep is not weary like a branch of bells; it is a microscope of the dry marrow of time.

:::::::

Slumberers are not weary of dreams, growth of the mouse in the silver mouse-hole, that marble was so spacious above them.

:::::::

The architecture of the mouse-hole achieved a turn of a withers of importance, that my fingers fondled the leaves of the palms with a sinking feeling, for the inner meanings or inner meetings of the sinking barrels in the inlets of the Isle. Therefore, what is my strategy or tactics with this Isle? So, the owls now would be sleeping, in their entire stride of a syphon, and with my long generations of dim fish at their sides. The fish howled at the so lucid cobblers of the dawn, over the valley the valley so slow, or the slow remembrances that were forged out of my dreams, and dreams now in a star-fire. An insurrection of the mallards breaks out of the crumbling flesh of huge white creatures, the zinc that the salmon sap up in this tropical night. I drew a picture in this place of shadow, with plywood views and mouse-hole views, or not, and I flung the gold and silver of bird-claws at this picture.

)))))))

## SIR GAWAIN AND THE 27 PURE SQUARES

Sir Gawain will be struck and crushed to death like some flea or midge forsaken far off in the gnawing venom of 27 pure squares to think of the long oars of a botanist who unlatches the latches of vulgarities. Nevertheless, Sir Gawain would crawl on the seas with purple label or green label for permanent revolutions in the consciousness of humankind, or to shoot a gun at the insect eels bent (shaking) with intent to prevent the overthrow of influenza down deep in silk. Gawain grew mild with spiritual changelings who ran from the seamless faces of Iceland that watched from the dire limits of lints or pre-lint to seal off the clanging tablets of oppressive murmurs, eeh! (the very strengths of which made several maidens move alive in my fingers). Gawain bubbled up misery as a saddle propels land through the lands in the wastes of the village of Shalott. Gawain, however, was dismayed. He would leave forever the immortal dimness of volcanoes adrift, and drifting back to me in the moonlit nights. He would leave volcanoes drifting back and forth behind me. Beautiful orchid or beautiful orchids, in the swamp-air, grew white as those lilies are white, among that weaving dark crux of the ether. The girl of the Tower had lifted her hands and wept, curls of a child, a silver child, curls of the child in cement, the silver curls, in my cold fingers, the silvery curls, in cement. I mounted the birds on my fingers, of the white fingers, remembering alone, all the birds of my fingers. Gawain, however, trembled to remember, the slag of nativity, the nativity of slag, or tyranny of 5 grocers, in the moon-lit night. Slumber was gone, for him and for me, and that wrangled all slumber, flooded all slumber, against the very moon-lit night before me. O white-houred Gawain, pure Gawain! if only 27 pure squares, manned or maned by girls in bronze canoes, with boiling epidemics, could move the beard of a young man to a red diagonal of conjurors, or lean on the wattle of a skylark that jambed against the expanding cosmos, the world itself would be liberated, cleaned, and transfigured! Lost in thought, Gawain became deaf against sweet slanders.

## SACRED AND PROFANE DANCES

A dancer looked at me with sharp intent, so I said "Age after age of these acrobats have fallen or fled while these poor crystals ('make') myrtle or ('make') a melon instead.
:::::::
Rage, rage is the light of a boy's love as the jelly-fish may be proliferating on the wet clay." Thus a jelly-fish drifts and dies, but with purpose, like the wrinkle-stone on the muzzle of a broken ox. Does a mere dancer in a dance have purpose? Then I would go quickly to murmurs of an absent grove of laurels, or to victories of islands out of forgetfulness in the horrible divide of the froth of the dry beeches. All dancing is empty of power, empty dust, and empty of powder, and shaking profane momentum, whence the cowls of the mercury of fossils. "None will know," I said. "None will know." A dancer twisted the valve of wine in a cavern. Though he was unsettled with the darkness in the wine, he then twisted the valve again and again. This dancer was most contented with a brash weeping head laid on snows, or the snows in themselves under all the dragonflies. Milk(y) as smoke was round us, and underneath us. Suddenly, a dancer set off his bombs in spittle of a turf-bank as a mob of dancers mixed inseparably in a surly and distant gallop. The girls of a caravan banged a hen while the wind and the sea poured into the clangor of the dance. A thin coupon drifted onto the womb-like yew, only to drop down into decay, stuck among obscure stones.
:::::::
"Stone by very stone," I said. "No, stone by stone in a dark tower," I said. "No, no, stone by stone in a very dark tower, as my straw comes trickling down, as a kind of asphyxia, that falls to the seaward way of the feral dance. I picked up those last sausages as night and then day goaded the tapestry of big moon with my kidneys backward to the aquarium. "Perhaps, though, everything will be overthrown," I said. "Yes, maybe everything will be completely overthrown." Cutlery, and less cutlery, make wool before my eyes but the fat capitalists have taken all the wages, for the scrambles of vesture, but this thin sky is not mighty (not mighty) under the war-men of the time.
)))))))

## THE VENUS-BERG AT THE END OF TIME

Venus and Tannhäuser saw not a sea's edge the same, and the wolf storm the xylophone the same, wrapped around them for adolescent pity or for child-like mercy. Milky foam was pulsed underneath them, and shaken round them, like the pulses of all waterfalls, or the pieces of straw thrown out of the barns on the gray prairies of the sea's edge, like the pulses of the leaking bees and wasps among the swarms of locusts and rice over sand on a prairie of birds and sand on the green of the grasses to clatter all gas in a washer. Venus herself, moving, as though the fit double of the landward mountain of her love, flits and scrapes the wood of one old woodcut before Tannhäuser, like the dripping of men longing for rest among the cubes of a heron of vinegar the sweet or the sours of that vinegar. Tannhäuser looked around him but immense trees grew taller beside the white lakes. Old silence had dropped a murmur in the gray rainfall of tangle of view. Weasels refused to live there, where Venus imposed a silence on the sighs or the murmurs of rain. The weasels fled in quiet horrors out of the mountain cave of her cold "love." A saddle for Venus, a type of harness, revolved brightly around her abdomen. A dog, in the mild warmth of the cave, was cowering away from the saddle. It feared the prowess of Venus with incandescent cotton. Thus dog and weasel fled, and other dogs or weasels followed, from the old sentinels of Venus and her mild theorems in the cave. Venus saw the desire of immortals in a chink of equilibrium in a rover on the chase with an enormous plunder of seaweeds over my finger-tips.

:::::::

Tannhäuser, ballad-singer, splintered a slide of tears or sweeping verdure of molar as crayfish after the warmth of lips with Venus. Tannhäuser, the wanderer, fled ivy, and hours rolled long in his riding the spine of the preachers that mourn spine before us, his dripping hazel. Tannhäuser fled from the mountain cave. He sensed not a sea's edge the same, or the wolf storm the storms, or the xylophone storm, the same, wrapped around him for all adolescent pity or for child-like mercies before him. He would be pulsed forever by silence, seaweeds, loneliness, and tragedy.

)))))))

## THE FAIRIES WITH A VESSEL OF SOUR CHERRIES

Anyone but Antinoös and I were lying down beside destructive muslin lit by the dim sheen of a blackberry under that stanza of ashes. Nobody but Antinoös and I drank wine from the skins of otters, dry skins in the patterns of a knob of the muslin kidnapper.

:::::::

Antinoös and a rough friend drank from huge cups that lay upon the pincers of thirsty raindrop. The lips of Antinoös, in their day, resembled the shelf of a lingerer by a wild crane, for he was happy with any lingerer in the wild. Otters slept on the heaped-up skins of the fairies with complacent knuckles, but when saffron steeped the sun in eyelashes there was a wrangle of eyelashes throughout the golden air. A wheel pushed out of the deep of a flagrant love on the rump of the pavement of a lullaby, or was it more true that lust on the chips of the pavement of the rump of this terrible twist of lullaby was ultimately experienced. Sleep itself rolled without an inch of love or much anger, over or simply under the contorted and naked confederates of Antinoös, displayed in their masculine flexing and tension. Very strong dust or strong dirt worked against the very exultant leaves in the night air, but the fairies held and chopped livid varnish in the belly of the wilderness as corpses of the fairies dripped to a sunken shape while a vessel of cherries was surrounded by moist foxglove in broken and chopped splendor. When the fairies tore out a tree, the tree that revolves with bitter slack ankles, the fairies lunged up in plumy fire. Shapes of brown then set fire to crayfish. "Throw it, throw it," the fairies shouted, "throw that fire!" I threw the slices of fire through a wave of my heart and spine, looking at the fairies in the shimmers of that night, and the waste of the bittern sepulchers.

:::::::

"Shudder," I said, "empty of hope or dread, shudder like pebbles in the kelp of textiles." Nevertheless, those fairies came carrying meat for a ceremony as I puzzled over the orthography on the red ceiling.

:::::::

The fairies and Antinoös were healed with unguents out of a broken rock-garden. Quilts were placed on the floors of the room where a shrine was feeding white moths. Quilts, and mirrors, fed on fairies.

)))))))

THE DESPERATE CONSOLATIONS OF BOËTHIUS

Boëthius, know the wink, speaks with a mind of lightning, to the thorned swan of lumber, as if the thorned lightnings mattered in the day or in the night. The fierce winds are begging on a so nice body of stones, with a crust of declivity or traction. "Be still as!"

:::::::

Boëthius sinks, a mallard ousters the shale in the thunder, among the wriggles of a fallen siphon, and the fallen wriggle, with fallen siphon, and fallen fallen. Boëthius hears these loud sounds amid the noise of the thunder. "Be still!" he said, for he would destroy midnight and dawn and sky with his boring philosophy. A small horse then loosely tears at the senatorial toga of Boëthius. Thus, this horse tore the wet toga asunder, despite a thimble full of the thick-stalked radar, or the horse clash and horse shock as horsey laughter through the geometry of the overarching bracken again before the mist. Ravens, however, look at a flock of power birds that taunt the other creatures in the vineyards. A red porpoise in the sea beyond, and in the silver morning, sounded like a cadence of death with mournful trombone as it feasted on a fourth of the insects and other animals coming out of the vineyards. "Be very still!" Boëthius said again. "But now the Barbarians of the north would murder all the lying priests, for the phosphorescence that is encased in metal funnels. They are weak men, and break their flatteries with barren galloping across the dusty plains, as lockets become worthless gifts in voracious galloping. I am powerless in this daylight to turn the beak of a snowy owl to a very white land.

:::::::

I summon mechanics with wicks of gully, for the wrathful wings of blackbirds within a flare of waltzes of teaspoons. Barbarians have left the path for all the preludes of hairbrushes in sunlight."

:::::::

Boëthius clings to the very snow in a storm where his progeny were burnt up by frost and ice. "The Ancient," Boëthius said, "knows that progeny alone is hopeless forever! Much seaweed crosses over a staghorn! But, I, a blind man, restless, am never still." Another blind man lies on the anvil of the torture room, as a winkle of buttons touches a yellow patch or a patch of red and yellow buttons become a mere winkle in the sound of rain and thunder when a poor thunder is choked with subtle rainfall.

)))))))

## OBSESSIONS OF IMMATURE PSYCHOLOGISTS

Daffodils close up the rectangles in a hidden garden under thorns as dark as blood the ripples of pigeons in my finger-nails but only the exultant daffodils will decide my fate forever. I join sleekness of the joiner of toad the joiner who stood trembling when a dank blade and a white blade shone in the sea-surges of the grim or the wings of the pigeons whose hours of tendernesses were gone then to eternal mathematics. I yelled for a paddle to paddle the circular mathematics in my thorny mind, or in my finger-nail mind, or in a daffodil mind. I told the pigeons to hide, so hide without hope or fear, as the grime of the willows weighs down the grime of the wet weathercocks. Storms died under shadows of the merry opium as arches of a squadron of insects tumbled down into the monologue of mentalist obsessions of the immature psychologists. A fight ate the dirt around a killer hawthorn, or did the fight shake the dirt, or did the fight circle the killer fowler, or disturb the ore of chemical dirt. The tumults died in a loud crash, so I could look upon some dreadful sight. Confound the chemicalized dirt! Twist that dirt in your hand, turn it between your fingers, and in mine! Green voice climbed ever into the sea-surge sky. Green voices will climb ever into a loud crash of the chemical factory in the immature psychics.
::::::
I held a gun whose shine accelerated the babble of tillage, and tiny words ran out to the dim orange colors of the thumps on a broken parchment the parchment of names, nothing but names. Shall I so broken then look upon some dreadful sight? I touched the printed names, the names of real men, who in a deep discontented pool did drown the jack a' straggler before my very eyes. Hostages were sent dripping to a croak of a tunnel to grapple for the cabled salmon, wet dark salmon. Folds of the sea built a dark hall out of a thin twine as honeycomb. Green voices cried to all the roots in foam or the tread or treads of pigeons in the mud. I am become the master poacher a master of the poachers, through gannet loops, not loops of a gannet where the faces of the turning daffodils will be as pale as fresh milk.
)))))))

## THE DISSONANT MUSIC OF AURELIANUS OF RÉÔME

Music, when buried through a great door with a thud as querns ride off on the slight thud of a violet. Aurelianus was standing at that door, but then came in, glimmered on the floor, with a spider's-web as it assails a pale light. Music journeyed round the halls of this pale light, like goats that howled or chewed on the thumbs of Aurelianus, those very bright and conformistic thumbs. Music, raucous, was found deep sunken in a brick wall, vocative curls at the wall or green curls against a bridesmaid among thousands of stacked doors crumbled beyond a dim prairie; but "Four" was the number of the prairie! "A palm-tree vomits clocks into the shivering night," Aurelianus said. They made a bubbling strain, for the blue screams of the oars and the gnats, on the stony and bare edge of silver turf and rollercoasters. "My music would be as dry as a purple withered sedge for glucose as glucose moves," Aurelianus said. I, for a strange sound, or for the stars as stars, the rhythms of the much larger constellations, am speaking to myself in pure but unknown language," he said. Vowels become the sowers of coral and the thumping of the ancient clocks, with torches thrust between the slimy pinnacles that a consonant was starving to reveal. However, the music of Aurelianus, made out of endless carven flagstones, followed a humpback cyclist as he turned, and moved, and turned again again beyond the old turf-bank, where shadowy jags flowed into shadowy jags, and six weasels cast down tempests in the self-same place, round a squall and round the varnish of the squall, all trades looked down on a tavern peacock, hour by hour and the higher dome, a wave-length of leathers or wave-length of hummings had been humming at a mule alone. Pillarless, multitudinous, the music of the maestro Aurelianus sounded like crinkled ailments in a teapot, the mob said. Thus this composer waited, and the very leisured rabble threw amethyst or sod at him as his musicians sighed and hoped for better times.
)))))))

OEDIPUS AND THE SCOTTISH GIANT

I desire to refuse the very notion of planes in the wet sky where hope is a demon for fright. I refuse to travel through the primitive narrows of the Isle of Skye to jabber about riddles in the night, Oedipal riddles with tobacco smoke in every vagina, crafty as the sea to mark oil-cloth udders. Oedipus sprang under a hazel tree to shiftily grenade vaccines into the shrouds of the Gaelic graveyards. Nevertheless, I need to see and endure the human collapses of human tissue on a pistil the garden rejects. That pretty pistil, pretty Peggy's pistil, is an angel that drops in sleep while topknots rage at a spider. I refuse to touch the demon of a mournful string, pure and complacent, everywhere, as the so mournful strings of the sad wrangle of migration destroys thousands of children.
:::::::
Is migration itself so dreadful? I am wounded in my precocious pity, but flee while liberationists may flee from cannibal tyrants throughout a world of cold and "practical" politics. Several wave-lengths of yolks fell into the Gaelic graveyard on the Isle of Skye, as many ruddy moths looked down on us from a blistered sky. Oedipus splutters with a red harness as the drapery shops are tied together in the light of a purplish moon. (Those shops were tied together with a water-rusted chain, for kitchen veils or kitchen bulbs.) The cliffs are full of ancient or humble eagles, the pips of the dice or sunset, on my mind. Gigantic eyeballs, out of the head of a Scottish giant, stood on either side of the rowing of a kill of fir-cones. My precocious twist of pity, like dry flakes of the scum, was seen on the feathers of the disheveled eagles in the daylight.
:::::::
Then I would touch stillness in the vinegar of a sloetree, as a dim turn of my pities, a very dim familiarity with the ancient things, like the dry kernel of a swimmer's chop. I would bring deliverance in a pale goose with a scapula of water-cress. Neither the Scottish giant, nor the very unlaboring Oedipus, will understand the vastness of the throw of dice by the random spiders, as chance-operations, for the pale goose alone.
:::::::
The Scottish giant, who never lived, may live and fight for tomorrow. But would it be for power, the total power of a faint penis in shadow, or the slithers of a cypress in broken syphon of a trout? The giant will decide the question. His household itself would destroy the goodly air!
)))))))

## THE RUFFLED EYES OF TORY ISLAND

I hobbled slowly along the glimmering sands of Tory Island after sunrise. A simpleton felt for keyholes in the sands, thinking of noodles I suppose, beside the piled-up mists and weathered rocks, with his outworn and then withered hands. I saw pigeons at a silver gallows, among the island's rings and the island bindings, that nourishing borders might truly socket under me for comfort and warmth. Men in the distance were fishing out of the new high-tech long boats, as the turn of a hawk in the middle air slapped at the very hawk itself from behind, and with bending spray and bending raindrops, dropped against the joker with paunch of a stallion. I touched carven figures on the rocks and wood by the seaside as translucent steam itself blackened the fir-cones and the rocks together. The stoats, thin and fine, were eating fish, pass by a tremor or the toss of a refrigerator, since other animals had become the very gentle warning that Tory Island, in all its glory, is a cold, stern, malevolent, and forbidding land. The landscape itself refuses brother to woven brother, bog and hedge of mint-sauce like bubbles in the frozen mucus, falcons lit up by the old aurora borealis that abides in a lonely spill of shows of three mushrooms. Chain a pond as in the tide the ruffled eyes of Tory Island will so ruffle a soup of discontent!

::::::

"These people know not law nor rule," Billy Butler Yeats said. A mallard, though, might cling to slopes or peaks in the hope of some quietness. But no, Yeats had said. "Hold no wearisome hope for the burglars of land and tide, the very reptiles of time, fear, and the abstract!" The mallard, though, feared no folded morrow, as wind-vane sealed off a mighty aurora borealis upon a shore of wood chips and slabs. Ruins on the island, market fresh, repulsed the badger and the boar. Then the mallard flew away foreverever!

## ST. GENEVIÈVE AT THE RUSTY GATES OF PARIS

Attila the Hun was stretched out across the old drawbridge of the city in some dim meditation or ancient yoga. He was thinking of cabooses of veal on the dunes of the coast of Brittany. Blind eagles, purring in the bright sunlight, began to sigh as they stood on stubs of thigh-bone or a burnt stub of vellum. St. Geneviève climbed the stair to a remote high door in the old cathedral, with a sound of irregular pistons or the sounds of pistons of green fish. She saw horsemen in the distance on a huge basalt platform, pity pity blue, but pity the basalt apexes or the equally basalt suspicions. Attila held his breath beneath a pace of the climbing steps and then climbing again over all contented dead choirs of silvery boys and equally silvery clerics, those lines of the swells of a briar or the swells of the phials in his hands. St. Geneviève, at a stone by the old drawbridge, was clothed in a misty gray, lighter round her shoulders, which reflected like a chorus of separate monocles a burst of sunlight in the sky. St. Geneviève, across the drawbridge, will go or stand within the parameter of all the boxers who loudly protect a blue parrot's madhouse. She would drift or float into a foam-gray seagull under the enamel of the briar. She would strain a throat of her enamel under the roof of a stone incubator. Attila, leaping over the incubator, shouted at Geneviève. "I shall be pierced and drop and die," Attila so muttered. "Blisters of my skin itself will cause a pile of corpses in the moat. My very bulk, so, or then, will be thrown in the very loud tide, the mere covering of splinters on an idiot, for I am an idiot. Pearls or gems flee from weeping itself, under a stolen tress or the stolen bits of camphor. I will not be moved to pity by the fleeing demons!" he cried.
:::::::
Geneviève, ignoring him, put face-powder on the cowhide around her waist; with a jot of powder she shook firm and spacious buttocks, for the powder men themselves heard gnawing against tendon within and without her gastro-intestinal tract. Attila, in a free fall, flexed his wiry muscles. He, thus twisting and turning in the air, was mighty of a line of the very mighty geometric lines of wrinkle of the mighty carcass so out of that mighty style of the carcass. "Sign, yes, sign yourself a tiny mouse-like duck!" Geneviève said, "consuming oblivion with a frown, your earless nerveless men burst out of the heights of the Orient with self-satisfaction and self-absorption, wrapped in the things of the red unhuman superstitions and despots, mere animalism! Leave this old place! Leave Paris alone forever!" Attila quietly withdrew from Paris.
)))))))

## THE FAIRY ARMIES OF THE SILVER OR THE GOLD

I invited the sprinkles from the stars but they were marred by many a great door within the milligrams of the verge of sprinkles. I broke from a long pole-axe the very wasps that ladle the continents to our minds. Those wasps warred between the twitters of a flagon or the pearly sides of the flagon itself. Old green pillars fell and crushed a mass of seaweed into the lace of the fireside that the mechanics had set for the wasps. Light alone gives a phosphorus of surge to beads of the wizard. Then I chose flight for countless pathways in a dark drowning (the drowning of Antinoös) as a technique or the whistle.
:::::::
"Left" and "right" were abstractions shining on marble steps (oh so slippery!) under the dances of the shafts of a crab. Then and there the tide glimmered (over and over) over the dark statues and under the pale words of oil-holes and incisions. The lids of soft Antinoös, though, were seen between dark thrones of water and mud in fatty sensations of coal and tar that yet held the incandescent rays of the seaport behind me. I will spend time, time itself, among the purple glimmering flowers uprooted beside these panels of burnt cypress.
:::::::
I wove my hair as very masculine hair (in spite of the dark towers in my mind) that gobbled up mussels and rituals together. White surf then gleamed in the darkness of a rose, with the skeins of wrongs of the mariner. The armies of silver and gold, surely, approached.
:::::::
Their horses of fire screamed about them, behind the wart of a dry scribbler of the river. An island itself shivered, not knowing fears of a stitch of waves or a stitch of grumbler, until white surf stroked the burn of the bell-sound of sea-wrack. A foaming tide, named by sweet names for the raillery of landscapes, formed a wide fan in that very water, whitened afar with horror, and with defiance and revolt!
:::::::
Will they be broken in pieces, and trampled, like the ruins of some ancient civilization? Will they be broken in pieces, and destroyed?
)))))))

## EAST OF THE SUN AND WEST OF THE MOON

I will be close to Antinoös at the time of the Apocalypse. I will be close to him, as I whisper and sigh to a desolate growth of a sarcastic wince, or the pearls in a muscular sprint. He heard the storm in the older cereal of the stammerer of glass. He shakes with the cold walnut, without the pity or the restraint of minerals, while a chimney still dreams of battle among the melting of the frost crystals. Antinoös breathed a portion of the ore of the air, or heard cries of the hounds in the milk of the fortune-tellers, a milk become concrete in that old dream of battle. Antinoös and other sad creatures, or hounds, are apart in the grassy places that float beneath a colander of nouns, that tremble and sigh until they exhaust themselves or are completely exhausted by the whispers of the Apocalypse. Where do I trouble the least of the drizzles of a surveyor, when all the drizzles are gone from the map of softness of a boy? I extract all the mud from three drain-pipes (fish fish for sole) so as to die in the tenderness where the sun in a saffron couch tingled a piggery of tingles and thighs for the pearls of the silver couch of the moon. A handsome fortune-teller was blazing half in the sea ways, and half not, that became nothing but pails of crabs and scrub. Then the birds painted a blaze of polish of manure on the splinters of a sturgeon, and words of the birds came over (over) me like drops from pails of an unraveling shrub fainter than the bleats of young ravens. A prospector held a wax-taper, and then stirred up a blaze of the leggings of an ogre. This fat ogre, though, was spitting his foul spit in the house of the poacher's lap, for he had over-lingered the welcome of days, and was lost. A somnambulist walked quickly to the edge of a staircase, and stopped abruptly. He fell, turning, with cramps.

## THE HOBGOBLINS OF WARRENPOINT

Dobby Bobby, a nice goblin, returned in furls from a dead changeling's broken jennets, and the furls the stains turned in his hands. Blue Burches, another goblin, kicked booty in gulch to an umbrella. These imps, wept of war were on it a hawk or a wildfire, kicked mounds of this wildfire or hawks on the mounds remembered how the Presbyterian minister stepped in shits for Warrenpoint. He saw flies everywhere but not at the brabbler of his own intestines. This minister walked along imaginary prairies bedabbled with red bruises and a spring-tide of silver-white wigs. Blue Burches, jump over these wigs, was equal to grievous chance for a surf of a wedge of mummification, until Dobby Bobby softly came and knifed downdown, but spoke no word, slice up the pale whimperer on a grill. "Many times I save a name or two, in one name or one-thousand names, the names that fall down into the ditch, with kettledrum!" Dobby Bobby said. "Two things devour my fish fin blues," Blue Burches said, "other than a kettledrum, that most of all I hate the slithery tendon of magic on blotting-paper!" "Pray!" Robin Roundcap said, "Fast or pray! We will then find a magnifier of burning old gravels." "These were ancient fates," Blue Burches said, "a watercourse will growl and growl again over a green bracelet loosed from a gate that morning tears apart before the tinker and the fairy weaver to lie in wait on one silhouette or other." "Terror," Robin Roundcap said, "simple terror is found in a bowl of oatmeal!" "Yes," Dobby Bobby said, "I stood by a shore of twists of strychnine on that minister blotting-paper, out of the numberless burns of aviation or the burns of these listeners who touch a staff of wood or a staff of wood-foam!"

Encolpius drank much wine from the pain of the burn of fireworks. He faltered before the weariness of a mouse, as odium flowed from the stoop of his hard body. "My hopes and longings turn to balls of dust and fibers in my mouth," he said. Timbrels of the tropics, dust from the hinges of the timbrels, the dry magic of the tropics, turned and fell in the tunneled wrinkles of his mind. He thought of forces in the night, sharp forces, as the naked infantrymen and mercenaries marched on the road to the north, far to the north. Softly dew dims over the roof of the golden villa of Ascyltus. Giton, a lover, pushes to destroy all the links of sentiment in his mind. "When Encolpius shall come from the arches, or from the asterisks of the archaways, the sea will drop down from the uproars of a small raven in the sky whose reptilian hinges have faded like a pale crustacean that simply withers away away," he said. "The solstices of lizards," Giton then said, "for Ascyltus, and the muffles of those solstices, with the rosy mufflers of the lizards, shall sigh sigh at last of the deliberate misery of the urinary tract of a poplar-tree for lizards and asterisks." Then Ascyltus and Giton kissed, deeply, tongue on tongue, as all shadows called their names, indeed called over and over again. Encolpius ate several convections while he cut voids and slashes in the vestments of a priest of Neptune. Giton then played in the sun of the starlings that dribbled down on the cold statue of Neptune. Giton looked at the statue, there and here, thus here and there, but around at the dry faces of the old servants in the villa. A luminous barrel of a very oily substance, turning and turning in the garden, kept exploding when a swift brightness was done, the blemishes of wood on the form of the parabola, along in an ancient whiteness. Ascyltus sent messages on a slaughterous twill, past the birds of water that were climbing with sad difficulty in the old Asian trees, the tremblings of course for the blue blemish on a cedar. Giton sang and sang in the clear sunlight of the garden. "I like the tulips floating in the air, a swallow also moving in the air, turned or turning my abrasions under the warm margarine, or the gentle waves of Neptune's tiny pool, orifices ready for me as I will place a golden ornament on my penis." Thus Encolpius sat down in the open pool. The servants raised their heads to the further twisting of adornment by Giton. The swallows became a focus or medium for the bronze tongs that were placed before Giton. Then the gladiators murmured and murmured at last for justice and truth, truth or justice.

## THE MORAY EELS

adeste fidelis the rainbow
adeste fidelis & rainbow rainbow
i seen a thin boy sittin' on his hunkers
automobile the faigh-go-baile in crest
wine & vinegar to andesite the O'Toole
under my andraditic O'Toole in the humid
& raw andantino of the Andaman Islands
there's hair on bamboo & stone as par
bid me to live, as clap clap
& go backwards in a taxi
the andabatarian anarchist
that was decent of him but now
i write an Ephemeris of the Irish saints
as the queerest explosion to explosion
the mournival of saints & knaves a thin
young man was welcome only in his bed
with my eyeshield & iron mask
password & bun of bath in nightwork
& where the where is your amnesia the
brine white suds of the Holy Ghost
or the milk white suds of the Madonna
under the land of god the land of god
in luminiferous Iraq
the iridial war my Iraq
the irideous war my Iraq
the whirls & quavers of Iraq
the warbles & trills of Iraq
warp of iridescence of Iraq
the trilineated whirl-worm Iraq
the mother-of-pearl of warbles Iraq
the whippletree of trillado Iraq
to the crippled friars the
ghastly crippled friars
& the sweat of Prester John
with the bestiality in Irish songs
true, very true, very true true
not fit to throw guts to a bear
with the holy Willy & costive Satan
or with the antedeluvian buffaloes
my deary, the lovespots on your hands
entrained, to shake the mounted foot
make walk a holy Willy & the
hobblesides of the hopfrog god
while the thin young man was shaving
the triumph to tell of past beasties in day
the unknown beggar comes to bigtimer
& the Moray eels are on the prowl

## DADDY GOOD HERRING

usque ad mortem
the four waders
& culpable happiness
pranqueen pranqueen
mark falling stars a lamphouse
please stop Moore's Melodies
ton & chin daddy alphabet
big beggar for chessmaster
ginargo for mastery over Tammuz
the five marshes & a marchioness
cyropaedia, hytospes
struck out in pencil by
a palace revolution that
defecates on the king
the belle boy of Nabomdo
or the evil Merodach
treckle trickle pharis for
the fake Mary in front of
a pipette of eggs & legs
or the pipette of legs & legs
& the egg magazine
& the 5-egg verse
the egg of the sleeps
as Rev. Jonathan Swift
defecates on the verge
while the boy Jones in
the cage of the lanternhouse
sees jinnies through a telescope
tip tip the Kate tip ad sum
Abraham Lincoln the rainbow my
Tristan sees the rainbow
& the chute of the sawyer to find
the paragraph of the rainbow
Walpurgis-nacht my lads my lads
the magazine-wall & artillery
good red herring in Edinburgh
or the clock or clocktower of Eden
Walpurgis-nacht under ale under
ale & Kennedy's bread
put the fish on the table
the bridge of good herring
& pass the fish to pass the fish
under the O'Flaherty & the fluter
de profundis de profundis
in the hollow of Christmas cake
the suds for me suddenly
the suds for me O'Sullivan

## THE SIMMERING OF THE TEA

or the skin skin an empty
cavern of skin over short shins
the flint off the glaciation for flint to
walk the mud like a neanderthalic ghost
or like a neanderthalic herd-boy in
the round of rounded caves the flint
the hypercatalectic flint &
the microlithic schillia
eons & eons of schillia
the schillia of flint flint &
the microlithic shilling
eons & eons of shillings on the
terricolous isles of Scilly or the
scilla on the isles of Scilly that
hypnotize the terror of a lisp
in time & time in time & time a
time that mocks for my grapes &
the ferret or frame of Fra Diavolo
sanctify, sanctify & tumble
with a terrier on the flint
the gothic flint
the sinister flint
the nidifugous flint the
sciamachies of flint
the spinster flint
the primer of flint
the Sivaistic flint
vatican gush a look alike
primarily, tell me all about
the scilla on the isles of Scilly
the eons & eons of Scilly
tellun tellun the pipette of flint
but sanctify now the flint of peace
& sanctify all hope of peace
with hunx & epheu
or the cap of a kidney
gestures in mutton & chaps
O mourveen avoure & avourie
telephone ache a tea simmering
the Turk moves in a theater
hundred manhood the hunt
& sidle to a shanty the
ankh of the ankylosaur or
the ankle of the ankhorite
steamy in the glue & gravy
pigeons, no concern
of the baronesses

## PIN TWIN FIN-FIN UNDERLINGS

& yum-yum a peach cobbler the
death dreams in a swanswong
the elucidatorials of the pea-pods
capitular pentmark on the beach
sanctify, sanctify, tumble &
sanctify with all my gracies
clear in my hyperborea
clear in my superboria
code code for us all
everyword for a self
found heathen by private hopes
the tongue in the old nickety
the milk in the sour pastry
as i am crossed out in ink
but sanctify, sanctify the
beautiful presence of waiting
for there be many asleeps
between thorns unprickly thorns
& dinna forget dinna forget the
terrible ugliness of Auslands
when i am crossed out in crayon
by the pin twin fin-fin underlings
waiting & waiting for cakes
as the huts revolve in the rain
sanctify, sanctify & tumble for
i hope soon to hear close the
turning & turning of milk on the
gap between the gap-world &
the new gap the gap of the
crumble of flint of sanctification
i touch the urn of a soft nose that
fumbles the letters together the letters
for a real foot twister of a letter-book
sanctify, sanctify & bumble the
arabicized bisons but bisons nevertheless
the pelts that are pelt-pelted on my back to
suck suck the brains of a boy of Mandalay
or the slit in the break of a psycho mandolin
i ignore the collapse of the soft nose of
sanctification from the earth though the
kill of the deer sanctifies nevertheless
the rumble or monstrous fire defences
the dogma of flint & the
dogma of effervescence
my toes apart on the flint
my toes are spreading, &
my pectoral murals the skin

## IN BEAUTIFUL PIETY

shake out the sound of frogs
& shake out the water in a spring
the hydromel of Keats alone the
saturday wax of the hydromel
26 blackbirds in 17 circles when the
black knights will shake out the bonfires
Hmmm, but i remember the plain of Bray
& i see & see again the plain of Bray
crossed out in pencil as the
sisters' wood refused to serve cars
2 white buffalos accompanied my doves
i don't think that was very nice of them
a blackbird sewed the truhite & the gould
when i saw the likeness of a saint in a wall
& the bleed of Moravian apples
the lashes & yells of cyclists
& paper & ink that started smells
shake shake the trumpet
& eye the trumpet or eye
the fish purr in beautiful piety as
the riddle of the telescopes
the clingers to Agnosis
determined by the babies
the agnostic puddings
the agnostic fir-greens
determined by the babies in
the majestic white of Agnosis
or the bald women in Agnosis
as the chopped-up meat took a drop
in the jetty of the river Liffey
shake shake the carriers of the Liffey
or the carriers of semiotext in
the moonshine of an ash-tree
take a chip off the old flint
with bald archaeologists the
avarice & restraint of pralines in
sonic avarice & sonic restraint
shake shake the testicles of flint
& the handwriting of daisies for
the news or tasks of Sinbad as
he punches at the 26 blackbirds
a chorus of oats from Hemania
or a chorus of boasts in Hemania
so now to our duck-and-jenny show
to stop the duck-and-jetty blow
write & read vice averse vice averse
tumble the odor of the apples

PORTERHOUSE STEAK

you & i developed a series of boils
our heads were x-rayed as the soldiers
dragged their fine cables to stars
neither the mustard nor the pepper
but the mustard and the pepper and a
turning of the worm signed "yellow tea"
annoying the soldiers the soldiers
referring to marks on their faces
the marks made them sorry sorry
one soldier was rambling in his speech
right to the very end the end when he
threw the contents of a jug of beer
the systematic cruelty in front of
the babylonian servants of god the
war with the long arm of coincidence
my wounds were consistent with bites
the calico body with agonizing sobs or
calico bodies of the sunburned mob the
legless boys engaged the mob's attention
under a cloud under a black(silver) cloud
we perspired freely among
the lotuses of the lotus-pond
in our Mandaean imaginations
our blackedged expressions
what could render my spiritual comfort?
overtasked by my own strength?
had the Mandaean servants of
the lotus sunk to the pavement?
the Arab prisoners offered no resistance
sliding across the valuable paper
the valuable paper of the desert
with commendable wrigglings
this war is thoroughpaced
& the Mandaean towers
are a temporary edifice
duffer or the duffer & duffer duffer
we put tweed on the war
as a sad circumstance when
the shape of face altered my
face that was formidable but
i was looking at a bottle & i
couldn't lay my hands on the bottle
or touch the hind legs of a horse
as a soldier ate a porterhouse steak
in front of me a steak that
spoke to his having seen death
to the best of his recollection

## THE SPLENDID PRISONERS IN THE CASTLE TOWER

Antinoös trundled down the steps of the
castle and Ascyltus trundled down the steps
of the castle and Attila the Hun trundled
down the steps of the castle and Aurelianus
trundled down the steps of the castle and
Frederick Barbarosa trundled down the
steps of the castle and Blue Burches
trundled down the steps of the castle
and Dobby Bobby trundled down the
steps of the castle and Boëthius trundled
down the steps of the castle and The Old
Butcher trundled down the steps of
the castle and The Corsaire trundled
down the steps of the castle and
Encolpius trundled down the steps
of the castle and Johannes Scotus
Eriugena trundled down the steps
of the castle and Federico Fellini
trundled down the steps of the
castle and Sir Gawain trundled
down the steps of the castle
and St. Geneviève trundled
down the steps of the castle,
and Giton trundled down the
steps of the castle and Hesiod
trundled down the steps of the
castle and The Morgana trundled
down the steps of the castle and
Oedipus trundled down the steps
of the castle and Pretty Peggy
trundled down the steps of the
castle and The Scottish Giant
trundled down the steps of
the castle and Robin Roundcap
trundled down the steps of the
castle and Tannhäuser trundled
down the steps of the castle and
Venus trundled down the steps
of the castle and Billy Butler
Yeats trundled down the steps
of the castle into the night of
my liberation or the sunrise of their own liberation.

## THE UNSILENCEABLE BELL

hanuman langur will be sinister, remember
blood of the mallard is
ancient waves, bitter pounding
the hanuman langur the old
wickedness of black wet leaves
maidenhair ferns are symbol of
death white white, voice of
light blows away the word

mallard mallard the unsilenceable bell
what is poetry? a fisherman said

mallard, hanuman langur, maidenhair fern
weight, i remember the sequence, soaring
stars the final condition, the
astral rock is to be broken

a new concept of, and basis
for, human development has
become an urgent necessity
i am an anarchist because the
future is implicit in the present

hanuman langur, mallard, maidenhair fern
foam is not a sigh, cloudy
dark robe water surrounds the motion
of two trout, eyes become
drained of fluid, drop by drop

the unsilenceable bell

sky, light, the color
of lemon, between
trees, light streaked by
light slender brown, the
mallard was looking at it

## THE CRYSTAL SHOE

bare body floating on surface
of the water, weeds of
water between my ankles
between my fingers, a lemur
will be creaking as the
water wind, rolling, rides him

lemur takes the crystal shoe

tide, shadows, music
i pursued the sound
not foam not lungs not women

but the ebb of animals
poetry & glimmering
behind a black turnstone
my toes are like claws, bird ponderous
my mouth is dropping

the lemur has a clear &
pale body, creature & growth, i
encumber, lemur, mindlessness & maintain
the lemur quivered to
woods foam in the heat

lemur takes the crystal shoe

cold light drifting down my
throat, now the lemur has
vermin & water weeds in
my long hair, brown &
green, he does not fear
disease, he pushes the stinking
river muck, black bulk

## THE LEMUR OF THE HOLY GHOST

jackal began to hope
again, wind crowd, elemental
trumpeter swan filled
temple blood well, riveting the
flesh, drops, to altar stone
the swan discomposed
leather, air rushed round her
wetness of the rushing, the
jackal rain, jackal wind, like trees
disheveled, remember black rivers
my dream, jackal jackal, i am
content, the jackals are
merely decorative lilies
the swan is confused, disturbed
i had thought that
dragonflies were the sun
i remember a saxophone

short legs & long body, stark
pattern of the skin
the lemur of the holy ghost
body muscle & mind, hegelian spirit,
inseparable, embraces the whole together
clarity is elegant, but overwhelming
appetence, immersion, fascination yearning
trumpeter swan will
destroy these walls
the lemur of the holy ghost

fall down! jackal jackal
flesh slain! jackal jackal

body triumphant, ambitious, feet &
stride enormous, the swan loses
self in the moment completely

## THE BAGPIPES

cloth next to the body
wind sound horses, eyes & bones
rock drip is mirror of druid chant
ferruginous hawk & red-shouldered hawk
an otter heaves, druid chant loneliness
dripping, from the black waters, the bagpipes

mountain, mist, shadow brown shadow
lips are sad gaze, lips
dragging the otter in
foam white mountain moisture cool cool

the spotted bull is warm, mild, trees
are trembling on the white bull
blood was the wetness over the otter

ferruginous hawk & red-shouldered
hawk creased into the
world pulsation pulp, they
roiled water wreathe, along
the veins, fat fat

the otter tears at his
own pelage, teeth are
yellow gray, pain screams out
my huge skin, skin reflecting
now the color of amber, & pale
the white bull rushed into
nothing but grayness

the bagpipes trembled against gulls & dippers

## LOHENGRIN

sirenian cow sweeps violet
cities through her brain
the cow was never plump
the cow slips into the
slime slippery hollows of her own body
flesh cavity sunken, reverberated basin

lohengrin skinned a blue hare
writing is the dialectical surge of
image against image by which the
cosmic falsity is poised in contrast

cow will be undulating eyes
elastic medium of pulsation
lohengrin skinned a second blue hare
articulation, sunlight space, was
moving, was gracefulness & formality
beauty spacious intelligence

sirenian cow, in
reply, rubs against
great jars jars
lohengrin skinned a third blue hare
he is languid he is calm
he is like dark deep honey
body suggests intense
compressed motion concealed
beneath a costume
of skin & fat

## THE BUTTER OF THE BRINE

druid will be shrill
careless power & careless brain
fox & badger in a stupor
i see existence, core, as
things unappeasable, & a dog
shouted & barked
rock insatiable animals will
not break, desires, teeth &
skin druids, are unfilled
the butter of the brine, arctic
shrew & cinereous shrew

bones of the druid's face are as if
hewn out of splintering beech wood
forgotten vesture, sun, hidden, burns

i am drowned there, a
dog-man thought, image
reflected on the water
a fisherman loosens out
hair, long & crisp & phallic
druid is mauve mild beast, he
is purity pale beast

the dragonfly world collided with
fat, & fox & badger lurched
a moorhen ruffled her own
tears into facial mask painted

arctic shrew & cinereous
shrew, rotting teeth &
self self-drinking out of the
pond water, my thighs
were bulbous branches

## THE BEETLE

the tree kangaroo makes a gesture
the dragonfly plunged into river

morning moves down asiatic
hills, white & red sand

but australian gulls &
dippers, & a beetle

an electrician's
writing illuminates
as it devours *
skin shred worn
body shards blackened &
broken, saffron &
red, torn by the
tree kangaroo
brittle fragment

i love all who are seldom beautiful
skin will be scabrous, allay
the irritation, rub

beetle beetle field "j" long &
fluid burrhel salt, the
sun is a blank now

tibetan burrhel tibetan blue
feet are red, sunlight the color of peach
tree kangaroo is observed, in
courage, resilience, energy
exuberance of her nature

## THE CATAMOUNT

between my ankles & ribs
pressing into every
fold of bleeding
skin, the catamount
is massive

ecstasy, leprous color
pearl pale, brooding up the
spine of the catamount, spine
that flattened to apple wine
night like milk smooth quiet, willows
by river restless dripping wetness
whispering cloth & body spread, dragonfly
& spider, limbs tenuous & tight, eyes &
sweat ankles shank & jaw ribs, grappling

surrealist plover's beak is a rose

there are weeds clinging to the
catamount, he swims, he is
fish cool, i touch his limbs

the plover, or catamount

a rose, moist red iridescent &
dripping, is little fire light
catamount, long red withering
body, hanging down, realized
the corruption in the
woods, deeper than
the warm wind could
penetrate, at the moment

## THE OX

the ox is heard, waters
of its veins & ducts are
a shield before the sun
i stopped writing, the ox the
marmoset the earth awakening
antiquity inside a marmoset
sweetness as a slender stalk &
lacings, celery leaves, frill

z & Z look, astounding dimension, poise
of the world & sunrise crickets crickets
body fills the field, marmoset, & a rattle

i stopped writing, the ox the
larval bees, & grave-robbers

wall pillars /bending /polished white rock
marmosets are as deluded in
their disillusionment as in
their primal illusion
my fingers become shadows of
desire, having lost motion exertion, crystal
& liquid upon the plane of
polarization light traversed,
rotatory twisting effect

## THE PREACHER

bearded seal pushed her
slowly lips wailing on
river water gentle, lips
of silver skin in closeness
light from the sun pierces through
the mesh of petals which
is in moisture falling

mirror is symbol of universe matrix of
heavenly dolphins, bewildering
reflexes, convex projection

ibis & bearded seal

ibis-killer remembers the
burnt citadel, silence
the preacher was
ingenuous, k "k" Q moves

swollen images rich in movement of signs
mist "k" unfolding the rose white petals
body is a cloth the color of topaz

architecture of the preacher's body
is determined by the fat
line of the lips, fat &
folding chin, full fat cheeks, round
smooth neck, heavy shoulders &
hips, features very small in
proportion to size of the
body ibis & bearded seal

## THE EMERALD STONE

bittern fell boring into woman fat
sundown blood foams dragonflies & dolphins
sky is green green cormorant green

the zebra will be
rapacious dream dark, chambers
of the brain, echo
the rose shines like ember to
hurt muscles & skin, torture

my toes were tangled in sand green & yellow
music of a body, motion, heavy motion

saxifrage & seaweed, the emerald stone

zebra drags the light to the
bottom, he shudders & pulls
then the bittern set
herself into mirror against
mirror heart, stars
are the weapon

alder wood, her head is mask wrap

## CHARLEMAGNE

charlemagne is
fishing, & wading
he bites cold hard the fruit
sand is floating in the waters
the pribilof shrew now is scarlet
maidenhair fern, the brown lizard

they leap against the
yellow waters, lips & lungs
charlemagne & the black-footed albatross
charlemagne & the pribilof shrew
water mother, cold, creeping, in
her veins, fingers & sweat, bone
battering bone, limb grinding into
limb, skin of the raw fingers decayed

what is falsity when fish think
it is truth tends to become
truth just at the time fish
think they have discovered
it to be falsity

the albatross is now
quadrangular, cringing
charlemagne & the pribilof shrew
charlemagne & the black-footed albatross
moon is shivering weapon hole, the
water in a gather that folded

charlemagne is
shaking his hair
maidenhair fern, the brown lizard
lust is a small
bell, murmur, low, harsh
interspersion, trouble body &
sparkle to the eyes

## THE PERFECT SERPENT

silver fox pressed petals touching
skin grass texture moist &
warm warm, & body, & the
manatee, crying among
roses forced & grass
the brow of the manatee
is like sheen of bronze

in warm warm water
the body of the manatee
was rolling over people
but the fox careened to
the eaves of his own bone
disillusionment & dragonflies
are connective tissue between
the falsity of symbols

my body is
fruit, leaf red red
fetter, i said
the manatee was
rhythmic stiffness, even
deep, avaricious
into the brain

flower pale person, pale as
hands of the other person
manatee, & the perfect serpent
wall after wall to the skin
eyes white night, anti
seducing, anti enticement
manatee, & the perfect serpent
to lie upon the edge
of sky, over sky

## THE DELECTABLE MOUNTAIN
## & THE SILVER MOUNTAIN

the sky is morning violet, darkness & light
dreams alone give endurance & power of strength

however, the merganser is tossing in
the wind, motion & body swaying
brain is tortured by shadows of
brain, water is a throne

the delectable mountain & the silver mountain

black-footed ferret struck, & water
reddened by blood, under the
pool, the rose floating, within
layers over layers of the yellow water

but what are these mountains?
they are the last mountains, the very last,
or a metamorphosis into something hollow!
& they are silent mountains, completely silent,
full of bubbles & words, thrones, i don't know,
that's all language, there's nothing else,
until freedom, my brain, until you find me

septet of silver pillars
symbolize the dualistic world

to be sure, the ferret scalded &
huddled skin, she withered in a
flexure, wisdom itself is consumed
listening to the rain, the merganser
is vast, the merganser remembers
the wind, black black trees

ferns & mosses, & a boy
lips move over his own
hand, succulent, shakes

## THE BLUE COW

the sea otter perished spittle fur
& sweat, within tough bright leather
the body color was mauve "s" "b" pale
the otter, bull wild, pulls out of the
water, legs dripping & teeth gasping, he
slashes his own feet, hurry

Z's paws were
tooth fire, edge
fierce & ravenous
the blue cow

hermit thrush meditated upon the
action of sea turtles
sea otter is thinking of epiphany epiphany

the thrush poked at ferns & mosses

eye cohesion, clarity & sensibility
splendor * fibrous * of the blue cow, wild
beast, multiple splendor, unity in diversity

"w" walk, fragment
blackened, skin is
red & yellow
crocus herb, yellow
body & yellow sky

architecture of the mind is
determined by impatience, aggressive
personality, distress, power &
depth perspective alone reveals

## THE HEARTH CAT

the rose-throated becard
screamed herself into
skin entangled by
ice, she cleaved &
bolted, sighting moist
the hearth cat hurled eyes clash
& my mouth she painted now
the body of the becard
is like stone stone warm
love, stone sheep & barbary
sheep are decorative heavyness

all my symbols are falsity
o Becard, image alone is true
skin skin thread pattern
delicate, & clear color
artist's drawing, destroys
geometric pattern weaving
rose-throated becard was
carminative & stimulant

the cat frightened the
stone sheep & barbary sheep
my body is a wall, multiple
dimensions, many colors

stone sheep & barbary
sheep were moving, but
in trance of wild retrogression
i am torpid, the flexure in rock

## THE EGG IN METAL COILS

white white body of a
woman, lying outstretched on
the water wood, substance
& spirit clasped in
gnarled branches, loving him
they are creeping in
the sunlight mist, under
& over each other

the woman thinks of otter &
stoat, & in the swamp of all
sex, stoat & caribou structuralized
& hard, it was raining warm
they bend nipple &
love, clouds, clinging weakness
muscles are wires
the caribou caribou

skin is touching the hot sand, the woman
remembers the trembling skin of summer
the egg in metal coils
the egg is dabbled & lean
the wind is quiet now

the woman never thought of a ferret
a bobcat brawled weight &
throbbed, mark violet with veins
he stamped & thrashed &
decreased immersion, opaque
then the woman moved among
greenyellow boughs, wood
changes into claws

## THE MEDIEVAL DOLPHIN

unhook the brim of
the sky, existence drops
away, the goat must
quench the moon itself

wings tremble, i lift
the eyelids to look
at the other side
pleasure, poking the gravel the
warmth, thinking of the mixture

the medieval dolphin prodded my lips
against the ears of goat deafened
symbols depend utterly upon the
delusions of dragonflies about
others & themselves

vesper sparrow was terseness then
roar is flexible, strenuous
Z, flesh Cross, is flesh symbol
of man, man of flesh

goat & vesper sparrow look, epiphany
is only an animal among wild flowers
the medieval dolphin is
not desire, we stagger
& skin of goat pounded against
the anvil of the sky

## THE ACACIA-TREE

blue hare, & specklebelly goose
arbutus & heaths, & specklebelly goose
have you ever seen a
girl's white body? the
acacia-tree the acacia-tree
hand is an axe, color of bronze
smell of endless land
body smell, affection
consequently, rivers in the
sunrise light red red

the dragonfly, like oxen oxen
black oxen, crushes over me
the blue hare encumbers me, skin broken
to desolate veil, the blue hare hid me
however, the ibis
meditates, white
bodies in black
mud, can he smell me? the
acacia-tree the acacia-tree

night tumbled to a blossom darkness
the blue hare shakes
shadowy foam, at your
lips, my lips are moist
specklebelly goose bladed
her own down like a loose child
storm is bird water driven, the
blue hare broke into storm, mirror
is burning now, a rustling

PARZIFAL

parzifal in the wood, where
bronze gong shivers above him, huge
heaven is black pit, the zebra laughed
i could crawl inside being, because
naked, crawl to the root of trees
dreams even are destruction, &
flesh drowsy pulsation to zebra

mouth & hair, melting bones blood gleam
in the bend of the moonlight the
shivers of a moorhen

the red-backed vole
was wakeful to the
touch, birdlight, bright, stared into
yellow eye of the fire morning
parzifal quenches thirst, his fingers
become thorns, the zebra pulled
back from the irritation

the moorhen struck
parzifal & a mermaid
the mermaid lay down, body waters
dwindled, & she became nothing
but feet, light feet feet

the red-backed vole
is pale, wind is
like the wet hair of the
dragonfly, black trees

## THE PANTHER'S BREATH

body stone of cormorant rolls
over & over i would yield to
the impact, body is like rock warm warm
hands are unappeasable thirst moon mother
rain is dripping through
the trees, i remember the
trees, that are dead, like
pole pale ivory, gray green, kiang shouted

the dolphin is tender trembling body wires
kiang is kissed, hair is kissed, he
floats, kissed through fluttering
& long haze of your own hair
water west, leaping, later consumes the
sun spiral, teeth & eyes, embers of
light forced through dull brown yellow veins
the cormorant is sleeplessly
loosened in body

i remember nothing but your white
skin, the dragonfly moved suddenly

bones of a lover's back are like a
carved door to the touch of her fingers
the panther's breath, saxifrages & seaweed
the eunuch & the sexual dorado
are like wild beasts

## THE STONE LANTERNS

i see the stone lanterns
breath in flutter, wind in
gray shaking, heart heart
is a wing to the wind
the yak is draining, the
slight graze in touching, into
every fold of its own hair & hide
you & i touched the stone lanterns
the yak gave a whip of kettle kiss
the yak trusted the
birds of the steppes
[metamorphose] the yak was wrong
the yak is now equally wrong in
being disappointed with wild birds
all characters were interrupted
all character was interrupted
i see the brain of the yak
the yak is tall is not tall
my confusion is visible

yak was cavernous
smell fresh [weeds]
the stone lanterns
yak moves through
thick yellow clover
& meadow meadow bloom
body bowl of silver, clay red red
& toes & eyes, white pearly spots
on your throat, hornless desperation
i metamorphose the stone lanterns
i metamorphose the yak

## POEM OF ALL MUSIC

Honor is tiger deep
the cavern of trampling charms
the star joy fierce
and a razor of water over
a Wound
we drink the lizard sense
and gazes

Listen to the ugly sweetness
of all music
the treble deep tone of world roll
we burn we burn the
wavestring sky changes modulates

Quiet is filled up by ice
and silver clutter
within the sealight (pause clear
and pause again)
all music pierces sight
the brittle starlight and
sky's crystal winter purple

## SNOW WITH OUTSTRETCHED

snow with outstretched
hands poised
for abyss unreaching

and yet languid
your body this deathbreeze
pushes

to an end
crystal before my
liquid eyes

remembered the
summer
moon reflecting

off level beachsands
they too were
shiningcovered as frost

snow with outstretched
hands poised
for abyss unreaching

## THERE WAS A FEVER IN SLICES

there was a fever in slices,
whispers to the skin, to whom
memories on animals gave
a golden shift

change valued the eyes higher, base
and the parrots emptied weight at
every tooth's prism, the fire ran
from its image every
time language drank from heat

and when peat-moss came to die, logic
counted up the bird-bites in its
own clouds, left breath gladly to
brown rushes, but not ice

signals and prayerbook powder sat at
the royal ice's skin, the
yellow expanse round winter, in the
lofty ancestral fever yonder
in the fluid by the blush

there stillness stood, the aged bite,
drank the last petals of sunburst pewter
and threw the sanctified frost
down into a bird's gut

wings and potatoes saw dye fall, fill, and
sink deep down into the steep
the ink closed, shrubbery
never drank another puzzle

## THE SMOOTH OBOE

the packet of a transmission is
like pumpkins: balloon comes from a
calendar, a herd rises to a jewel
and is bound to return back
to the sparkle's moor-hen,
alternating everlastingly

the pure tongue's stone streams from the
steep crystal, then, in a trance,
all clues turn to cloudy barricades of
owls against the smooth shadow, and, gently
received, creatures undulate, veiling
caresses, questions, walls, and
softly murmuring, down to
the mutton and mulberry

if mirrors stand out against a
fence's descent the reflection foams
angrily step by step down
into a blind jump

in the even elevation the lichen steals
through the trumpet's surface, and
in the smooth oboe's map all the
lithographs joyously mirror their contour

all worship is a delightful segment
of the arrow, gesture mixes
foaming chess-games from
the jaw's ache

## THE HORNSOUND SNOWFLAKE

The abrasions were shining
so golden, an ashtree
was standing by bleeding
blackbirds at the bracken's
grime and heard a cormorant from far
away over the quiet daffodils.
My earthenware caught a ferret
within a fish's gill, and glow-worms
thought secretly to gunpowder
beehives * oh, how
herons go along too,
in the radiant jam jar!

Two young jugglers passed by
on a leech and a lemon,
as magnetic jelly-fish walked
through the quiet mallard, the
marmalade heard moths and mint-sauce
singing: of dizzy rocky needlework where
the nipples rustle so softly, of
nutshells which plunge from paraffin into
the primrose of the quicksilver.

Radium sang of marble raspberries,
of reptiles which run to
the red-shank bird in
twilit corn ricks above the
naked saliva, sardines in scarletless
salmon where sedge and scutch-grass
listen at the lobster silhouette
and quartz milk silverweed when
the hornsound snowflake of the
spume awakes, and the sturgeons
purl sleepily in the
radiant teaspoon's tendon.

## THE WILDERNESS

we are compelling
the chain of
sunstressed wilderness
the tyrant sun jade gaze unquiet
mighty to be divided
the old harmonious birch filaments
the grief slab of blackest basalt
(we were in pain but we
were not in pain)
the grief slab of glassy basalt
we were spongy or pumiceous as
we broke the porphyritic olivine
we linked the cataractal maze
of whitened elements
the serene slide of river water
the rule of worldless wilderness
the catchless keepless wilderness
the byzantine convulsions of the birds
we struggled ocean wild grey beasts
and gentle yellow groves
the swirling steady pace of pain
the tame riverslide

## TETHRA

Tethra,
god of the dead,
carried
her
hidden
in the tiredness
of step after step
while the
point of anticipation
lusthung sharp
in her body
until
her ears
caught
the glad cry
of lichen-covered rocks.

As greying dragons, they
faced ragelike the shadowy
rippling waters
with their greenbreasts.
Tethra crushed her
head on them.

## FIREFLY AND SEAGULL

brush is following a bronze guru
to the wavering molar sunset
to a heart by the long ravioli to
policeman of beautiful whipped cream
to popsicle dead in
a leaper of caterpillar
to weapon eating wild
waltzes from a carp
to cyclone playing
in celestial feather
and to that dark cubicle
beside a braided rug
of youthful feathers singing
to the glassblower

when the octopus comes
up castaways will
live at lemons
covered with cavernous
shells, and sparrows

and wrapped in a
sea of lost coal

but compound weeds are
coming to the horseshoe
and squares will
be vibrations in
a musical firefly
in a bowl of burning feathers
burning like a
rosebud of the amoeba
pouring its sun
into the lunar seagull

## THRENODY

i spread swiftness into
the manysided multiple mirror
i imaged my skin as
sky sea calm the
monstrous bright shape of
disjunctive melodies reflected
in error cavern

life (like the mirror) is
multi-colored too the
breath of summer purple shadows
on the steep dawn
i scale the radiance of awe
and star weep depth
i embolden the sick
beast of white rosy smile the
cold cleft of rock
i am fearful of the while

legs of the bare boy
gleam in brown light
i pour the leprous orange
skin into an adamantine cup

## SONNET; POWERLESSNESS

i am graved as tower crag
the obelisk and black
multi-storied double column
i cradle cloud and snow
the imperious quicksand
i stamp the wrath white temple
strong and fire mud crowned
i am not solemn i am
palatial powerlessness
the forest is a seashine of
bladed bark and brittle blossom
the lively mud
at my breasts the
volcanoes of moist mouth
water the
waterfall force of
obeliscal azure and rock

## SONNET; A CELTIC DRUM

we touch
the slow whirlwind of
his falling figure
gathering cloth within Z or
we touch tempestuous a
thousand stormstreams
that splay and splinter
the mountainous edge and
rock tower this is
destiny tumult the sudden
roseviolet rising and blue
we sky cleaving cleaved Wedge
the dome split stone White
and speckled toppling jagged shattered
we desolate we pierce the
thin place in creatured sky
center up vomit up from
crack cracking earthquake crack
we inhabit in cracked creeking
and silverlightwater creek
we brittle split the greek rock
like a cube of ice

GHOSTS

within a quill
within a mandolin wind
actors castle and carry
all priceless dwarfs
mallards pursue their celestial
texture with flaming moonbeams
parachutists roll their suitcases
in heated geraniums, jelly-fish manure
earthquakes search for roots
lost in skulls, in mackerel
maggots pass over the
hexagons of wanton chaperones
the heavy submarine flames

tapdancers draw cannibals from
the eremites of blue eyelids that
burn through a communal stiletto
treasures loop'd and mantl'd to
the pessimist of corsets
murdered merchandise with
the fishes of hoaxes
and sweet scented ghosts
whose centers contain
crescents, teeth, a cello
fish lustr'd linoleum
and all the thorned mandolins

knuckl'd, become balls of quicksand

wanderers, beefeater, the wounded
kaleidoscope that cut through
a cask in kerosene hysteria

## STALLION

mist that sinks all
jungles into the fingerprints
and gurgles about the
huge moons in zebra
handcuff zebra moon eye dreams
of black beehive nucleus the
scroll has grown enormous torches
hidden in a stallion, in
stallion, in plasma of throne

reeds hammer'd and heckl'd beneath
the secret cloud of light, stallion

lantern-holders hiss'd beneath heated
beetles and were sold, halter'd
hing'd to many chemists' unicorns
to land on this guitar the
swimmer's cornflake mud
lipstick sails in a
war horse of brandy
as lakes are kept
within a perfumed baby
where they swiftly glaz'd and
glob'd beaches of jigsaw puzzles
twilights growl'd and gander'd
within purple wild stallions

gorge pens, gorge tophats
gnarl the naked miner the
necklaces that issue from whistles
silver only the unopposed cradle
of journalist these painted skies
watch only the reeds

## STONE CUTTER

Stephen Thomas, epic anti-hero,
Walked left-round
His house in
Bare feet.
Those
Short nervecords
Made his toes curl under.
Grieving dog had scarred his
Auburn-haired lip.
Agate cutting.
Taking the sphere (glasscovered) of
Poison-gas, he
Smashed it on the
Floor of the concrete hall.

After the smoke had
Cleared,
Fergal O'Hanlon
Saw the
Grotesque shapes of the
Dead stripped
Flesh and scattered among
Concrete and agate slabs.

Turn the guns
Against yourselves
That throngdead
From their graves, he said.
With a shot, Stephen Thomas
Did smash the
Rest of the world in
His mouth!

## ORCHIDS AND WINDMILLS

as the final turnstile of pinetrees pours
out from a banshee out into the
glue to watch the night begin
then a faun's slop will know
the destructive earthworms have gone
into the zither's bulldog when the
wounds invade our machines and the
skunks yell their placebo and suck
hard as the jellyfish is
lit up by magic orchids

my hydrogen spitting saunas
come to a ritual pathway,
wind and rum

machines leap over the sorcerer to
climb into wrinkles, violet walls are
crawling backward to enormous chariots
locomotives are ascending to the limitless
mistletoe of hypodermic needles and
into the crevices the eucalyptus tree
is following snails into the fermentation
of sunbeams and the horned sailboats of
a ruby, stockings have entered the
anthropologist where the dead
lizards speak to rope

the flat oxen are singing, and rooftops

and the graves of the swastika are
written in an oceanic sombrero
the mushroom is heard the leopard
despite the runningboard of mad
windmills the flat serpents are singing

## PICASSO

Overblight, all this,
in the frame of eye,
oversee (amber and yellow) that this
panic of the stranger
is a gibbet
sheltering you (self).

And more of whiteness nightly.
Rough rock and (kiss) snow.
Caulk me (you) and credo
the black otter.

Overworked by verbs,
wild, smelly, thankscolored,
what a black sheen, unsightful,
I seemed to be a verb, rank smell.

And the seanight of white.
Snow (sails) kiss to ground in roll round.
Over creed and caulked I
am the gulfstream lime.
For immersion in this endlessness forever
chalk Space/time.
Wither go coming and none.
You are the span of all flighting sleep.
My skin is green now, withering.

## LOVE POEM

I choke the pine, pine.

The irrational sun and
Sweet wind and wolverine.
I do not give a
Verb to the quiet.

Wind and bird, I cannot speak.
The throat of my love is
Large, throat shimmer and color of
Carrara marble.

Blackbrown valley is
Churned out of fresh air.
We are not fire fire (when?)
We are not spirit.
Do you have a name? you and
The afternoon crow?

You stand like the initial pine,
Spare, lank, sparkled,
Swaying in the dance of pine.
I crumble from your curly tall heart,
First growth, lighted joy.

I choke the pine, pine.
Bark and branch sing.
Leaves glissando.
Bird and wind.

I have become dark in the sweet
Sun and wind illogic.
Throat is an agate.
I question the wolverine.
I cease, cease.

## EELS AND CRICKETS

The zigzag is sultry
over the marble wren,
whose milky woodcut pranced
with a glowing wickerwork,
runs downward to the
vinegar's twitter, where untold
tillage the thigh-bone
with gently lapping sunburn
washes into first discoverable
sting the jewelled spider.
The round sodium turns and
holds within the smotherer the
sinews of old sea-gulls.

Each jagged rock-fish
of rainbow, no pinecone moves,
stands, and parallelograms of
stony mustard sends far
out where twinkle milk-pudding
starlike membrane crystallizes,
if on their pink crow's
nest zigzags the insulin slants.
Beneath, the merry hydrogen dances
and shouts, and on haddock
the gauze gangrene when
featherdown face-powder makes eggshells
look like eels with
innocent and curious crickets.

## POEM OF ALL FAITH

This is white rose red rose
Over the cathedral.
Nestorian priest cooks brain
From the black pig.
He is a good man, thin, yellow teeth.
He draws out of the brain a red-white thread.
(We dream the death of night.)
Under the lagoon, under the
Canal's black water,
Froth and watery pearls, the sky above is
Yellow smoke.

The Nestorian priest floats down wind.
Is he asiatic? Down the white wind bubbles,
His tight leathery red
Muscles, his dark muscles.
Tomorrow tomorrow the street is jungle.

We have moved to the citadel.
The Nestorian priest takes a black
Heart from the pig's carcass.
We enter the brothel, like yellow smoke
Distracted, the loose pinewood door,
Endless cloth taken from the pig's brain.

The Commandant of the tower is
Fleshly red-white embarrassment.
We are expressive,
Through the large loose door of brothel.
The Nestorian priest is young; he
Also wrecks dogs with black and
Yellow slivers of bamboo.

There is white smoke
Over the lagoon,
Red fog over the canal.
The Nestorian priest takes a rose
Out of the pig's carcass.
The priest is sweating.

## SONNET; HISTORY

i pass the future
in a space of icy cave
boy is wavewater tossing dark
and the man a delusive sea
mud and falsewater smiling
spread smeared and sinking
dropdrip sunken
i betray enchanted i betray
the sunken island that
revolves beyond my fingertips
the smooth water
and shadow double insects
flowing to
a serene day death the
lightning sun mist
the sun gulf
i am gleaming in the sunlight
the smooth water skin
the infant brain is a boat

## DREAMS OF STEPHEN THOMAS

There was a mountain of flame
    through the wild chasm of shattered
        rocks they called sky.
Dolorous moon had been swallowed by the fiery
    tombed-druid in the western sea.
I shall reveal my power, Balor thought.
His face was sharp and fleshless.

Who are you? he cried.
It was the end of autumn
or the end of deathsounds.

I am Domnu, goddess of the deep.
The wind that breathes over the sea
    screams my oneness with the Fomoraig.
I am the inmost being of the earth.
Three struggling snakes
    formed me out of their conflict.

These violent snakes formed a globe
    with foam and sweat
        from their bodies.
With united hissings,
    threw it into air.
I am that earth.
I was created out of their battle.

Look! screamed Domnu.
I see only the moon, Balor said.
No! she wept —
It is the eye of HornedSnake —
    who has come to devour me.

## SIX ISOSCELES TRIANGLES

I enter a tower. With seawater all round
instead of sand heat. I evaporate by the
moonlight the culmination puddles, the
primal water-buffaloes, the sun shape
gap crescent. Within the inner precinct
the tower. I produce odd sensations the
spiral and the loops evaporate. I join
up the spiral the crescent join up with
my fingers in sky. I descend the tower
descend across the green wheat the sea
sun. I wind round — round — quickly
the way, chunks of earth in the wine,
the mortuary mound. I descend toward
the sun water the sun river sole sea,
the wetness purple courted galaxy.
I — snake spittle sway — wait hopelessly.
There are more than six isosceles triangles
drowning in me. I am not expectant. There
are sand and water millions the triumph of
abstract form. The drowned women motion
— motion — to join them, the impacted power
the precision, the quiet comes from far away
noise from far away. I crawl into the curls
the slithering stem curls of sleep, the
drowned women inside shivers of scales.
The drowned women send out ripples —
ripples — to compete converging merging.
Into the tower the tower is made out of
bones — curled up — shiny and proto-god
the bones the cold logic the enigma.

THE KNIGHT OF DUNSEVERICK

THE BARD :
He was the Knight of Dunseverick. Into the body
of Déirdre. We bring slaves. We bring slaves.
Nothing! Nothing nothing is crawling over the
sky, the forests of towers — irrepressible — a
place of passage the long lake fingers of the
sky. The sky washes the bodies of women, the
cascade sky of mouth rock spittle skin. The
sky flows chips of wood. I sky the water sky
filled up by fierce rubber the dance marble
women. I am not — drift — drunk. I float full
the sky snakes and reptiles. I am not motionless,
with a dance boat bad boat, the dead women
decayed in the sky. The river sky and decayed
limbs full float the ever effortless passageway,
the eternal death passageway of the sky god.

THE PARACHOREGEMA :
Nothing! Nothing nothing in the sky over
sky washes the nakedness of men, the sky river
marble mouths. The slaves over slaves. I am
filled up, the dance drunk drift drunk dance.

THE CHILD :
Nothing nothing is crawling over the sky!
Yes yes! Nothing crawls on the sky!
The sky flows chips of wood!

## THE EUMENIDES

Embroidering thin face,
ah flowers at his feet.

Torches, like tendrils of the
vine, the torches, the vines.

Paintings, frozen figures, moving
against the glare the flickering.

Orestes, traverse the night.

Orestes, cry of the night bird,
the dismal bird, warm bird, the
throb of slowmotion bird, quiet.

Elektra, frightening yet curious,
the eyes gleaming, calm, smiling.

Lulling sounds, to the
murderess Elektra, the
paintings, a firelight,
frozen fire, the bird,
or paintings, a frozen
flickering nightbird.

Words flowing
in darkness the
gentleness, and
low breathing of
hidden Orestes.

Orestes, traverse the night.

## TRANSFORMA(c)TION

Melody, at night,
the melody, in the
lazy hot streets,
monotonous tone.

Beautiful music, the music!

Monotonous tone,
sunrise the red,
the consolation.

I am Orestes, reeking
skin, iridescent, the
reeking skin, rose and
lotus-bud, the bleeding
skin, most formidable.

Fearing to be seen, the bone and
murmur, ah rounding statues, all
rounding the statues, at the end,
the ruin, the mirror, all the red
rounding statues, the ruin again,
all reflection in the lake O red.

I am thin the iridescent temper
the water black marble O purple
and ivory-hard the animal eyes.

Murmur of the water the purple
shadow and carpets of red skin,
climbing and crowding the black
marble the shining eye over eye.

WAR

This is war's winter when the tree
Is broken orange and yellow.
We have spoken to the tree.
The tree does not speak.
We have seen the nothing sun, the
Purple twilight nothing.

I am unsettled by the small
Bright sun, the setting redness
And the point unsetting.
We are quiet. We see wild quick and
Quiet zebra in the blackwhite
Edge of knife. We are golden zodiac.

War, we hate your shrunkenness.
Curse this pleasant place,
War War we bless you.

I am a man of something,
Pushing in an ancient stain,
Brown and ragged, heavy.
In the strength of splintered
Bone and burnished copper,
I gesture outward by water.
I am a man of something,
Willfulness, dignity, I swim.

Unburied war, we are cold in the
Zodiac. We are the pretty silver
Vegetables. We are chiseled in the
Cold copper and tree — broken — that
Will be grey and metallic.
Waken waken, War, we
Chant the chaos in iron ore.

I am the winter zebra blood and hot.
I am carved and curled in marble.
War — distractible — is learning
Alphabet in the waters, public
Verbs that do not eat meat.

I, hidden, am a man of
shrunkenness and metal.
They cover my phallus with mud.
They hide my cowardice with fear.
But the winter red tree
With middle branches
(What is this envelope of
sudden orange and quiet?)
Reaches the folds of starskin and
Extinguishes the big sky of war.

Winter's war when the tree will be something.

BALUSTRADE

Don Juan
la crispation

une nudité
le mimétisme

Don Juan, Don Z -
figure de la fatalité

une nuit de printemps
aux cérémonies

secousses de mort
Don Juan, Don Z -

générations d'ombres
danse au clair de lune

le tzigane [tzigane]
la neige tombait

dans une chambre
d'un texte mystérieux

sous la lampe
Don Juan, Don Z -

merveilleux
les témoins

entre les fesses
des cercles et des étoiles

contre la balustrade de fer
de la géométrie

le fragment
aux ongles

dans le désert
précautions

Don Juan, Don Z -
l'angoisse l'obligeait

la séance serait truquée
le soir [le soir]

de la figure de gymnastique

## SALVADOR DALÍ

Muchos pocos hacen un mucho,
la cereza, el cobre, la cereza,
la cereza, cereza, el cobre.

Salir atestando, el búho,
el perejil, el cobre, el
cobre, la cereza, cereza.

Cuando la puerta es baja,
hay que agacharse — la anémona,
melocotones, los melocotones.

Hay un juicio, los melocotones,
cono de pino, ortiga, la noche,
noche, cono de pino, la noche.

Tiempo tras tiempo viene, la
servilleta, la mañana, la mimosa,
mimosa, la servilleta, la mimosa.

Zurrar la pavana, pececillo,
urraca, mármol, mármol y loto,
loto, y loto, urraca y mármol.

Llorar con ambos ojos, lagarto,
limón, mariquita, mandíbula,
mariquita, lagarto, mariquita.

Lo mas encomendado lleva el gato,
hiedra, serpiente, iris, serpiente.

BENJAMIN PÉRET

"Lo mas encomendado lleva el gato,
hiedra, serpiente, iris, serpiente."

Palabras y plumas el viento las lleva,
petróleo, agua, agua, herradura, agua.

La calentura declina, espina,
roble, casco, casco, halcón,
ganso, espina, roble y casco.

Dijo el escarabajo:
"Gusano de resplandor,
cubre de escarcha, paredes."

No morderse los labios, niebla,
vellón, red, niebla, abeto, red,
abeto, labios, niebla y niebla.

Mondar los huesos, haces
de leña, armiño, olmo,
olmo, alce, olmo, olmo.

Suceda lo que sucediere,
dragón, pan, polvo, pan,
polvo, pan, polvo, pan.

Salir de lagunas y entrar
en mojadas, cenizas, delfín,
cornejo, y cornejo, zarapito!

## SUSURRUS

i make a gesture to the north
wavering buffalo & wandering buffalo
a mallard returns to a stream
salmon were drops of flame
that hatched the
saffron morning as
the fishspawn came

tints of a horse the silver
creased & folded, rumpled
like a frozen insect
rum was tufted in
the horse's tints
death & time with glances

i am lost in foliage, a kind of celery
but it holds that flashing mallard up
thyme & sinews of rose-beds
determine the sunrise in the dew
guitar of piggery a thick guitar
with day's air the double negative
i see the paroxysms of the salmon
in a broken cup of river & rock
i am engulfed in the susurrus of insects
a ferocious herd of mallards approaches
my pile-up of the seeds of corn
i am purple, a sluggard
i paint my arms in the dirty stream

i walk away from a buffalo calf
silver silver the buffalo tints

the sting of an ogre
stirs all buffalos' horns
to the kiss of toadstools
the infant ferns unwrap a
powder of the drapery of carnage
the blackbird evicts a mob of
jugglers in the pollen that
cloys with the mallards
budding along the unwieldy sun
a tackle of orchids
that the planets run

## THE PYRENEES

climbing, i pass over the basalt
unto the starry mountains & mica
climb! to the terrible
broods of the quartzite
the throttles of a wild swan
flashed a glow that
bristled color to my eyes

the scarecrow of orthodox ritual
arose to the tatters of stars
pasteboard of the cubes of sails
across ruby cars of sunrise the
skin of the lipstick of doves

i rein in the slaves of liturgy
brightness of the dewdrops on a
spider, cold & methodical spider
i gesture with a bronze rod
jazz of a rock-shelf of twists
that holds an iron bond to the
sparkle of magnetic dewdrops
woven to each other

an osprey babbled to sling me in
all my listless hours of fear
an orbit to drown the spitting
but fear no dawning morrow in
phosphorus of tassels of mud
a gray osprey in sorrow
ice of the lemon of maggots, echo

i thread through the
threadless mountain woods
bound to return back to
my ever-simmering solitudes
the ospreys are devious & round until
the clacking tossing reeds grow still

a tepid dragon
upon a central hill
tar of cuckoo some tar
gathered in a panting
not milked by urinary downfall
flung on high each waving osprey

## THE QUILL AND THE ID

Refreshed rejoice all in Maeve,
with this day feast food, bodies
branded at the touch of swaying
weeds, under the honor of the
beaten Maeve, solemnity colloidal
and guarded Maeve moist, this is
colossus of bones and bowels.
They feel tomb dare.
Laliulay laliulay.
I am the remainder Maeve.
(I am priestess of the raven.)
Ruction to get into the heart
of Maeve, like the bone of a
word erect, the dicolated verb,
the core of bone selfness
worked Maeve royally.
She uttered glory.
All all guarded glory to rejoice at most.
She spoke a prayer to the dragon goddess.
Her words are empty sounds like birdsong.
Frightful woman, your words are dreadful!
What can I do now to save her?
Still beguiling as you face your death?
He quickly retreats, almost with a shudder.
What's happened to me?
Quill, and the Id to me is in amber sky,
and before you what broken Maeve hot
bone revolved and twisted over the land.
She defecated against skin, the turning Maeve.
Heart twisted. She undulated.
Nevertheless, she did not faint.
Fiber and cord of mellifluous demon,
the contorted cord muscle and part
of Maeve discord into portion ever
endlessness as mire mere god cord.
Maeve stalked eternal Uuum.

## THE LEATHERY UNGUENT

Flesh beside Maeve motion desired land.
Laliulay laliulay. Laliulay laliulay.
Virgin sent, these follow anguish sunset
anger bent, sequence torn and virgin
smelling sump to sacrament of pentacle.
They are virgins and these wither
follow dragon; she slow so goes.
Without muck they are like bending
insects before throne of the magician.
Oil effuses against the hair of Maeve, the
stain that is a verb emasculated, oils poured
to bend and worship, tricolate. I am Maeve.
Maeve is the name sounded action becomes a tomb.
Cúchulainn lowers his eyes.
The ecstasy of the new
brings fear of the old.
The Badb hands Maeve the cup once more.
What are these weapons?
She who here defies my threats?
The mist still flutters before Cúchulainn.
I will dry you with my eyes!
Word as a mere small bird.
Maeve poured out, she is
only the adolescent idea
of young men dilixerated.
These boys are delirious delicious.
Maeve effuses, twisting skin,
and the tumbling tortuous and
flagellant, body falling like a lamb.
Work me Maeve wondrous, after
you tongue push into skin the odor
of leathery unleathery unguent.
Drink me Maeve motion marvel, I will
run hair and skin against the swaying
oils, after the odor of power and tongue,
after you curry and press to brittle brown
ore beneath the ointment brain.

## A GOSSAMER FIGURE

Exaltation into the village of Warrenpoint.
Exaltation to be more, Maeve, tralling.
Voice is a bone.
Pleasure to be more in you.
We will be glad.
Maeve then then is a laying
light spot of yellow red.
Because with the brown fire and splendor.
She adheres.
Dare, in the end, to be spellbound!
We have been eaten up.
The Badb laid in his arms a gossamer figure.
O give me back myself!
Cúchulainn peruses Maeve, in admiration.
How she must be pleaded
with for something so good!
With lips cool as river fruit, I lick
the dialectical Maeve and she dilates
to me demented, ego dilectious.
She feeds and I, rolling, return devolving.
Lection me Maeve mindlessness yes yes diluted.
Maeve is moored in pond-water, warm, among
the weeds and willow water, sunset amber eyes,
fleshly lids, yes yes, Maeve suspended in weedy
liquid brown, limbs at strain. I am Maeve.
Submerged rose petal and
slime soaring lotus-bud
touch warm the eyelids
of Maeve pleasure.
Eyelids closed in delight.

## A DEPTH IN THINGS

Whorling and turning to
an eternal presenttime,
Maeve falters, falters.
That pastured between lilies.
Laliulay laliulay.
Turning and returning in a whirl,
Maeve then then coheres,
in desperate disproportion,
strain of muscles twist.
My heart is ready.
Chorus of the people chanted glory
of Maeve, glory of her orange dark
skin, parted core of magicianly
medium, thick and moist.
We will sing and salmon will
die purple red and grey.
Maeve is political power,
because pliable plants
become warm with texture.
What should I say?
Give me back my old self!
But his arm drops to his side.
He sees a depth in things.
He steps once more to the mirror.
What do I hear?
Maeve spies a mirror, goes
to it, and puts up her hair,
seemingly unconcerned.
Maeve pirated emotion.
She inhabited brown
yellow temples in her
time of stone blood.
Because the senses toiled
in terms of centuries.
Maeve total strong.
We will dwell beneath branch of oaken evil.
Maeve protected in quaking violent wings.
The noise that you are, smooth and dry.
You because of you. Extravagant cover
as an element of the whorling evil.

## THE BUBBLING WATERS

Cúchulainn clamors to verify the total
injustice of Maeve, deeply cried quiet
and heard them, when Cúchulainn (in
deliverance) dominated us to exalt by
the voice of speaking ease.
I am the undulating Cúchulainn.
(I am the other priestess of the raven.)
She smells of leather and pus.
Cúchulainn tribulated, and from
much troubles all all divided these.
We just cried. They freedom these
to selfness violet after fearful yellow.
Out of all overwhelming Cúchulainn.
What should I do?
Give me the undivided happiness of self!
The Badb and the Morrígan
take each other by the hand.
What's happening to me?
The bubbling waters melt away
and Cúchulainn falls on the shore.
Maeve ambulated calm, within orange
yellow magic massive, fingers formal
washed white and blue yes yes world
not be, hesitated throat not throat.
Every limb stretched and tense at risk of decision.
Maeve beheaded boys brown blood oblated she.
Before the festival Cúchulainn.
She fervored at the merit mud,
against the god rock.
Corpses beseech her, yearly, kindled
by their gladden dragon black.

## FRENETIC FLOWER VULVA

Cúchulainn spatial spiral in disgust.
Maeve sampled vengeance with her
fleshly lips. Out of all all ruptured lilies
are these paleolithic raw lips.
Before the tongued cave Cúchulainn.
Maeve artefactured.
With the sweetness that is alone in hatred.
Cúchulainn in justice clangor cried.
Bowels and bone cried.
Am I not still the one you desire?
Give me back my whole being!
What is this drink?
Precipitous women!
He carries a boy high in his arms.
How lovely the grief in his gestures!
Maeve, frenetic flower vulva, barbarity
in beauty, motion twisting harsh body,
in everlasting temporality, small belly
flanked long, she makes curved
medallions for liturgical domination.
Chorus of the people chanted bronze in power Maeve.
She incised.
Always praise these in silver and red mouths.
Barbarous cruelty is beauty copper curving.
She cut and she notched.
Slime skin reflective Cúchulainn
is then then in endless ever time.
We will bless the dominion Cúchulainn.
Laliulay laliulay. Laliulay laliulay.

## SLEEPERS IN THE CURRAGH

Cúchulainn groans.
Mouth is a fosse.
Ego elegy of clothed world world,
but Cúchulainn has eaten and
warm fruit afferated his stomach.
Out of the mud.
I have chosen.
Cúchulainn fructified in vestry strong
and silver bronze, he corded to defy,
he spat crude red paint against hands on
stone ceremony, elected metallic primitivity.
I see a curragh with three sleeping people.
The sleepers awaken in the mist.
Then the sleepers tumble over one another.
He looks around with charming astonishment.
Who are you talking about?
What have you done with me?
Get him away from me!
He fought against majestic Maeve.
He chose to defy her with utter magic.
Forcefulness is beauty yes yes leafy fruit shall endure.
They will lay hands on you.
Cúchulainn earthquaked horror in his brain.
Maeve pestilenced in quiet.
Cúchulainn perished hot sweet
dragon, dragging his animal hand
to anal Maeve, and not at tangent
these torments of touch after malice.

## THE BARBARIAN SACRAMENT

Visible are the insipid eyes of seaweed.
Those others are dull weed rock at rest.
I shall not touch them.
They seemed to die.
Maeve filled a sound for evil ocularity.
Cúchulainn in the sight, banded by
bracelet gold, he looked out at the
stupid brown sea, blue fingers graced
his own fat bird belly, his heavy hips
that rolled and plundered verticality, his
legs that loosened white, he creatured
thick face and flanked with dirt.
Cúchulainn saw then then the sea
as death yellow monster mound.
Cúchulainn opens and closes his eyes.
Quickly forget all the horrible ills of the world!
How you touch me!
I see grey eyes in white faces.
Then all inner disquiet will be stilled.
She is the bristling mauve Maeve, tainted tip
to the all all overwhelming cord of rectum.
Late and hairless to me now.
We who are filled.
Power power alone is beauty.
Laliulay laliulay.
Cúchulainn saw the adversary now,
contorted lips, cold intestines and rock.
Maeve is the sacrament of all barbarian society.
She saw a depth in things.
Brain bounden dragon now.

## MELTED WAX

Finnabhair is brought before the throned Maeve.
Fact is written by a horn sounded
monotonous pitch medium eternal.
Finnabhair struck a tam, she
qualmed her amniotic surge for
the burned and seriated Cúchulainn.
Liquid brown in middle
of the ventricles and
intestines consumed Maeve.
Brain becomes motion melted wax.
Cúchulainn is dressed in a shining blue garment.
He puts two languid arms around a cursed figure.
You are marred by the salt of the sea!
His arm drops to his side.
What have you done with me?
I'll run and fetch a bottle of lotion.
Finnabhair to make tumble is hard
against her own mindless boil of bowels.
She pitied the mountain Maeve.
In the midst of window body.
Then when moisture in a flow serene.
Finnabhair pushes yes yes to constant ooze of
zeal, she tortured the oils within the cow Maeve.

## VERBS AND ROCK WORDS

Cúchulainn in revulsion then became a
cruet of pale brown yellow seaweed wine.
Before the cave of intestines.
They will lay hands on me.
Maeve modulated, her verb
ornamented zeal, she counted
the geometry of dragon evil.
She venerated grey
and spotless short
against the subjection
Cúchulainn, she beguiled.
Verbs and rock words became
trumpeter purple in the bright.
Light shines only from an adjacent chamber.
I'll run for the flask with the blackberry juice.
Your warmth flows through me!
Let us accomplish what is meant to be!
Maeve clenched pieces of ice in her fists.
After all all adversity she was translated.
We have been eaten up.
When is bitter and hurtful
smell of zeal domesticated
to all comedic dragon.
Heart descended, it melted
within the trombone of amber
bowels, the imitation Cúchulainn
to attain, hot and word bone loud.
He steps once more to the mirror.
He seemed to die.
Heart melted like a molt of steel and leprous wax.
Heart strangled by the mud hot intestines of Maeve.

# THE SCAVENGERS OF THE GODS

Two crows, shimmering
like black pearls, hover
over the distant sea.

The eidolon devised from yearning
by our separate, dreaming façade
sometimes advances,
dazzling and unproposed,
into our very psyche.

But the specter originated from libido
by our further, dreaming selves
oftentimes approaches,
marvelous and uncalled,
into our very shadows.

I hear cymbals and clash, gloomily, the ghosts
of the clash. Though it is necessary to suffer
the almost complete randomness and imprudence
of selection, for that duration, theatrical duration,
the very archetype of sense perception, the very
framework of intention, leads to pure but subjective
nominality. Irreflexively, all theatrical figurations of
dispersing and haphazardness are fixed in patterns
or networks as far-off discord, and the persistent
effect of scattering is incontrovertible. Cruelty!
Hey, the gods! Hey, the cruel gods! The fish-men
and the scorpion-men guard the door to the botanical
gardens. The Badb and the Morrígan blow against
arbutus and horns as thin women are supremely
indifferent to the moon. The chemists are
covered with wire-stemmed bunch grass and
a low bush like Scottish gorse. Thus I touch
blemished figures, lunatics, revolving, with
stained glass in their hands, defective glass.
I put two languid arms around a cursed figure.
But grasped in the isolated form of its pure
motion, theatrical intervention, despite the
illegal appearance it assumes, in being
ineffective, ultimately functions in the
service of horizontalizing order, and
even, as Maeve and the Badb and
the Morrígan shall see, of anti-hierarchy.
For, doesn't the theatrical passage to the
global, the universal, and thus to the
goodness of infinity, impose a disjunctive
choice or decision in which the being of
the one will falter?

## STREAMER STARLING

This taint links cowls and orange pips
To the flashing snaps of mucus
With harvest marsh, and tiredness, tower

Heath between waverer and peninsula
Streamer flings out the orange of waste
Which (fish for plaice) splatters might,
In the flaming sage, take
Measurement for vaporous fangs

And palmistry, complacent boxers gruel
At the starlings of instruments
Can also pinnacle the yew sinking
From grocers and maze

The membrane of a brilliant pillager

Vulgarity links lakes and screams
Pastry links uproars and wrongs
To the flashing goose of swirl
With matted harvest melting-point
Digestion is heavy with brilliant solder

Sling minnows between vineyards and a jumper
Side flings out the eels and tubs
Which any metal chink might, in
The flaming spool, take for
Flying mastication and solder

And scrags, and starlings
Complacent rafters
At this woe of conjunction
At this wriggle of killer tissue
Can also carcass a tavern sinking
From a manuscript from
Exhilarating courtyards

## TENDON

These reptiles on a thirsty wax-taper
This orifice without a passenger
Stitch, mew, and the silverweed in a kernel
On this tress the qualms drown ailments in

The mutilation of the cherries
The flare of haddock stuck to wanderer
The intriguer (fish for perch) who
Carries tendon and metal away
In the silver of broken lips

This looking-glass finally, on the thunderbolt
Where flower-beds call music, and a whip
And the trampling watercourse the
Sturgeons and the interlude delirium
Of the bullock as a tendon passes
Snarl, the lard and twilight furl
And the station of a tendon in taper

Each herbalist lifts a watercourse to shouts
Octagon is as if several sturgeons trembled
While the aches of a windowsill foiled
The universe of rice, muzzle

Spoon geometrizes on thirsty causeway
The spider's-web without a yell
Consolation stub, and the mark of ledge
On the spider drowning itself in fuchsia
On the tropics the
Mineral drowns wigs in

Socket of eye of watercourse
The inflammation of the
Sturgeon in a swallow
Eggshells carry bellsound
And face-cream away
In the vastness of
Tendon and rice

## PIGEONS

within a wave, of vaseline ceiling
seaweeds masticate and carry their
priceless aquarium, seaweeds pursue
their remembrances with flaming eyebrows
veinslashers who roll their
hair in heated epidemics
imperialists who search for
locomotives lost in water
pass over the song's valves
of wanton cages the wind the
heavy submarine clouds and hiccups

overcoats that draw hexes from
the staff of blue fishline
udders that burn through
all rapiers as wolves
unravel lithographs to the
bananas of freckles
murdered buzzards with
the monocle of changelings
sweet scented flags of
bicycles as mosques whose
tightropes contain salamander rainfall

valve and follow their thorned confederates
unravel, become rubbage of rollercoasters

pigeons, phantom pigeons, shoulders

the wounded shoes that cut through
words and word in the urinary famine

the drain-pipe birches
the surf of refrigerator
while wind-vane twists a whin to a couch
blemishes protrude from panels of pears
as premonition splutters on a blistered
rook twined to a weasel yes a weasel
necromancy pebbles the progeny of
pebbles trickling out of a sentinel

## CLATTER TO THE MALLARD

Thatch symptoms of hissing and skylark
Where atheists begin the clasps
Of a whetstone, and the pony of hissing
The painter closes like an odor

And a gold quicksand
Slips merchants in bundles of twigs
Summit cress robs a
Zero and a periwinkle
And the ransom of
That false womankind
Linking woodflakes back
To a lamp-shade

Scroll, tide-mark, and these
Spindly statues twisting to
Overthrow odds and snorts in stature
These curves whose horrible clatter
Takes the vulture out of a mallard

All these patterns decorate
Querns and seasurges
As if with lava irregular shrouds
This mere chance of vaults, and shafts
Where wafers and asterisks float
Chattering intestines blacken the mallard

Morning machines the machine
Come to meet a shrub
Down the margarine of vitrified raillery
And the telescope the same as the pea-pod
Men are rowing a smack in a
Tunnel of humpback mallards

Anatomy rock-garden, and many mechanics give
Spindly twists to mechanize all tapestry
Balladsinger and speculator view the
Shadows of a mutilated toe
Conjuror at the windowsill throws
Lettuce and millstones at the mallard

## THUNDER

Misrule tomato of hooter where mortises turn
Cases and welder in which pillions burn
The sulphur seething with 27 fiddlers
Gobble up the sequel of rushes

Bizarre thunder milky thunder
Bubbles from the nickel-plate of grease
Bubbles up from the grease of visors
A lichen climbs and throws into suction
The pulses of the jelly-fish

Caterpillar and traction, the entire crane
Flings itself on goats in one willowy disc
A disc suspicion of primitive flange
Shingle and mechanics in fern

Odium of sprint where antiquaries turn
Splice in which burglars burn
The water seethes with slaughterous mitres
Gobbles up the extortioner
Of dyeing and kitchen

Milk! Bizarre cowhide violent straggler
Bubbles from a peacock of source
A foxglove climbs up and throws into winkle
The jelly-fish willow the thunder
The sorrel the hen

Prowess and convict, the entire
Tab of pewter flings itself
On silencer in one ether of wiliness
A skillet reef of primitive mash
Mashes the tweezers and twist

## THE FISH FIN

Meteors and rainbow showers collide
A gash is peat-bog solidified
In sunburn become maggot

The passionate weld of ink
Convokes crystals thrones in
The pitchfork heights of green cooing kinks
Around the marmalade revolves

Wreckage flits through the myrtle
Of the thick-stalked acid

Just one eyelash commands the vomit
While opium flaps on and on
In the veal the vaginal bagpipe
Places continents under a fork

Solstices of glass collide
Mounds and pigeons are crystallized
The fish fin is clear
In a pigeon become blemish

The courtly vitriol
Convokes ovals and twinges
At the swimmer's heights
Of green swabs
Round around the vaseline revolves

Hairbrushes flit through the scrambles of spine
Of quadrants and a mousehole-thick plateau

Swamp trembles just command a ribbon
While nostrils and wrenches flap
In the beeswax a vaginal scarecrow
Places a martingale under
Drawing-pins and rims

## TURPENTINE

Radius hears the insect yelp
Of distant severity behind a
Knell of closed whitewash
Thus, in the redwing the turpentine
At the teal of ducks in pudding
The jack wails among the lints
Of glazed paper behind terminal

Brief marrow jars the xylophone
Snows of a coffer have
Fallen on pavement and gnaw
The vocative, gnaw the arches of old reverie
Swells of a topknot destroy the rooftop
Old sprinkles of a fawn arch away
Concrete plummets a red knife
Among the mists of mint-sauce

Where is the magnifier wound of the scrub
The parabola of bleeding wart within a heifer
The wasps that kill a thick duck
The redwing that treads
Teapot magpies in the Z shape of locket

Meandering wool mourns on jowls of zinc
Humbled kittens sting volcanoes in dandruff
Style laments a hill on a ferret

Again olive-tree hears animal insects
Of distant rock-fish behind lungs and lung
Thus, in the vertebra scrounger
At the sodium of banner
Fish whim wails of the eagle
Stud rubber on fig and sedge

Brief fly-paper memorizes another venom
Nightmare jars and gnaws
The spindle and desk
Washer and laurel plummet a
Red stanza into the swells
Of glucose and fowler's mists

## THE ENAMEL WRANGLE

[cantus firmus]

In the flood-tide of full-blown beads
Where volume muffler breathes in a stronghold
The booty feels a spill
In oatmeal and tomorrow

Over leggings the wood on exertion
Uprooted dials pile the stillness
The enamel feels both a wrangle
And oblivion say tillage leather

For here entrails with the very wilderness
Of phosphorescence are on enamel
Stonechat bangs the equilibrium wrap
Of insurrection in a thorn, elegy

The drizzle curls forth from a nut-cracker
Like a poplartree or like a tinkle
With milligram fumes and waterfalls inside

In the looting of erosion sunrise
Where this whole detergent breathes in rein
The situation mediation feels enamel grow
And land in oration, yellow over yellow

Over espionage the thatcher
On riddles or vigor
Uprooted parrots pile fractions and ripple
The beetle feels both a kerchief
And influenza say bugle bugle

[cantus primus]

For here the throat with the
Very belly of microscope
Of wine are on cubes
Wrinklestone bangs the chimes
Of the lumber of wrangle

The beetle curls forth from a ripple
Like fractions or like a parrot's riddles
With wrinklestones and cubes inside

The waterfall curls forth
From milligrams of tinkles
Like a poplartree or like a nut-cracker
With drizzle, microscopes and chimes inside

In the armchair of full-blown jennet
Where a whole simpleton
Breathes deeply in falcons
Strychnine feels a candlestick
In piggery and twill

Over poison the seawrack on gosling
Uprooted knots and drapery shops
Pile sky-high in a croak
The amethyst daintily feels a bittern
And a teaspoon say rill

Here asphyxia with the very verdure
Of a horn are on the forge
Shores bang the bittern and the dewdrops
Of wrangle and of enamel
Seafarers bang a roe

## THE FRIEZE AND THE NITRATE

Macaroni of the witness, an
ornament's sleet (frieze of sleet)
still haunts the balcony, the nitrate,
bitter tenement, ammonia's ended
for a lubricant, and all cod,
the entire bile's afire
the marble's cape's being
drained away by the liver
and your mincer goes
gnawing away girling away
at the oscillator of a wicket.

Basket, basket, mutton swarms on
all over the proliferating jazzdance;
declivity of the raindrop, yellow filaments
ride off on toads, on gardeners.

Apexes rage, hogs twist,
the fireside flows into the
reddened surveyor like
nourishing furls, a nourishing
blue hedge; squalor and polish
dribble down now from all screws
waves, harsh twinkle and a sheen
of vinegar covering the embankment.

## THE POACHER

With a squall of bitter mackerel wicks
Shoulder-blade of some obscure yellow dot
Towels and sap weighted down
By a polluted backbone
Drifting between brakes and a piked fish

Splenetic doe upon black
Stripling of blood running blood
The poacher whispered at aggravated woodwork
Like the sputum and dray of
A tomb extremely orbited
Of the parachute of dog's mast

In the spray of brindled fish
Where a lobster was writhing
The summer locomotion
Held out tinges of oaken label

With all famine of a
Throb cobweb, vows
Of some pliers-held heron
Cavernous effigy, yellow taunts
Weighted down by a polluted knob
Drifting between a portrait and a thud

Splenetic joiner upon a water-hen
The piston grenaded an aggravated larch
Like the tattler of ladle extremely drifted
Of turret of sentiment, and a portion

In the incredible wedge
Where a paunch was ruffled
The listener summer held
Out a stimulus to the
Poacher with abrasion and alder

## CYPRESS

Again green earthworm plunders water-cress
And face-powder supplement
Of honeycomb and sod
Where the ringlet of dead textiles
Is encased by fumblers

And cutlery within the
Molar, mild serpent
Has howled with cypress of wire

Pouch floods, in that squint, the sheaf
Of corn encased in shouts of the
Monosyllable wolves of slithery texture
Of the mantelpiece, loiterer cypress

Pinetree and whitethorn marker
A strand with sauce in drifts
Wreath and checker tip a field

Again prowling green plunders tails and ribs
And walls up the latch and slouch O poplar
Where a sculptor traces dead
Barns in clay on a racer

And ousters within the blackberry, mild stench
Have howled with grime of vituperation

A dune collapses, in that
Sob of lambs, the crab
Spits out long timbrels of pearls
Of the intruder bruise
Stallion lands in growl

Cypress and crab vestment the deep
Skeins of janitors trickle dice

## SPLINTERS AND ECLIPSE

Voices, sowers cheat all orthography
Prelude sabotage since vesture splintered
The eclipse achieves a ware of skyline
Revealing crux and wheeze as songster birds

An oddment breathes among the prairies
A chancel comes from
Tin-whistle knows not where
So that the bays of all
The violinists are transformed
In a little woodcock without one splinter

Among needlework the muddy maize
Full with murders and a murderess
The tortoises lay down in downpour
Vogue alone splintered an isthmus
Dragon so low splintered all light

Murkiness seals off the meters
Of the planetary slit where
The luminous throng is whimper
For the crystal lingerer
And overarching lingerer

So here the weir has oars of daffodils
The graveyard briar and smoke, eclipse
The floozy verge in a violin of wine
And the colander with twenty
Avalanches of mummification

Fir-cone seals off the silhouette
Of the planetary splinters where
The luminous tornado is seaport
For the crystal fir-cone
And overarching fir-cone

## WRINKLE

O give a gannet coral of hot dizziness
Quilts burnt up by wrinkles of straw
Theorem canal the lucid canal
Inspected back and forth by mobs of pipers

Allow chilled owls a daisy under outer enzymes
Sifted over from wrinkles in a smirch
And let colored streams cross over toadstools
With incandescent wrinkles

Satisfy ghosts and octaves the
Wrinkles have a hungry pestle
For universal blackthorns
O pour spikes! pour a star's tablets
For vertex in moan of astral tablet

Detach all vinegar! divide a brown swan
With your rump of amputating turf
Close up all burning phials for oil-cloth
Where metaphor can out-descend mere wizard

Intoxicate the wrinkles
As a stammerer drinks from
The whimperer of pure steam
Ruins tear apart all throttles and plugs
In the convection of some
New powdered grumbler

Allow wheatenbread a sunset
Under inner camphor
Sifted out of thumps in a cyclist
And let colored sepulchres
Cross over frogs and sausage
With incandescent dragonfly

ORCHARD

Charter of the palisade, slag,
Potash leopard sycamore is virtue
Snowdrop of the orchard gargle warp
In snowdrop gargle warp, sweetbread laugh
& quarrel finally closing the speed-boat

Kennel of the rasp old cascades of settlement
Cove of ventilation skinners of a mosquito
Wrestler of cardboard & comma of oarsman
Squares of verve also luster of butcher

Adolescent linen, wolf & mercury
Frozen radar, knuckles & knuckles
Conformistic weathercock
Conformistic thigh-bone
Precocious detachment

Squabble of technique white infantryman
& finally again restraint reaches a gulch
Silver soup of a burning gown, ogre
Adornment sneeze of mussels, crag
Cupboard sloetree is stolen & soaring

Cabled varnish piercing varnish
The varnish is voracious the
Varnish is a stratagem a womb-like preacher
Turn tatter waist & delicious boils jambed &
Purged the orchard the snowdrops
The contractor walks on black snow
Rheumatism is electronic missile
Lilies, & this ankhorite whirring in a sieve

## FIREWORKS

Navigator the maw dwelt in stake
Window-sill on plaid mustard

Of burnt veins, of sea skewer
The aluminum where thorn-bushes run in oratory
Premium of witch and of pond

In the gadget storm
Fossils of seaweed in shale
Kidnapper, the punctures assail a blue paddle
Mutineer of a lighter all udders gleam
Savants flagon and window to the fireworks

Mud and pigeons fly
From the keyholes of market terror

Lime the lap in tongs
With onions and a mariner
Who warbles for a finger-print
With chop stile

For fireworks shall salmon cast down shrubbery
At the kelp of the sun
Make fetlocks and plundering thighs for
Salmon to intertwine

Flash for the marsh-hen

But maned by irrigation
Resin pushes down in the munition of sparrows
A sparrow's padlock plunders
A sparrow's terminus
On the booty of trumpets of a nun

Marsh-hen, for milk clot on a rifle
Heckler to a site in duel
Strings from a puff-ball that
Tripod over shells and bowels

## RHINOCEROS

as the final mistress of a botanist
windmill'd out from a clay crator
winkl'd into the pomegranate to
watch the waterfall begin wine
then trapezes will know the
destructive virgins have gone
into the violet wings when
the cabooses invade a spider
and the kelp whistle their
globe pain and wince hard
when the wildfire noodle is
lit up by a magic boat
a rhinoceros is spitting barrels and
depths into ritual larder and carpets

spiders that leap over the oscillation
to climb into a starving turkey
belly buttons are crawling
backward to enormous bottles

meetings are varnished to
the limitless webs of canoes
and into the word's board the
fuselage is following all skyscrapers
into the tennis racket of
spider's mud and the dragonfly's
horned sidewalk of pillows
swimmingholes have entered
the gremlin where the
dead daggers speak to starships
the flat panthers are
twinkling and twitching

and the brick and bricks of the
revolutions are written in oceanic snails
the baboon is heard despite
the gas of mad dragonflies

## SPONGES

Firearm raises a leech and a vixen
Of sensuality lost in sponges of beloved meteorite
Slats cannot hear the thin thicket

Thicket memorizes the mire while
Perspiration joined in the
Filings of palm-oil as
The grouse (final drawing-room)
Wagons all scissors away and
Wakens cabbage and adolescent skew

Summer does not listen to vegetables and catgut
The badger breath of scarlet everything

Become a density a wallop
Pinecone and wireworm oxide to tears as
Thighs float on a valved soap-bubble

Emolument burns off the
Valves of a gander as
Plasterers breathe in all
Herbage under the lifeboats

The plover lifts a mitten and a trident
While slate shades itself in tumbles of buttermilk
Stutterer is lost in the mitten of buttermilk
Buttermilk cannot hear the deep
Vexation of the beet

Phosphate memorizes all mirth the
Mirth of shaving-brush joined
In the tides of the eldertree
The cartridge of final speck
Nets swine and an adolescent flageolet

The village fails to billow as a
Dictionary models the end of visibility

An archer branches himself past the
Velvet, sponges, and rivulets on a wren
Crickets thigh away the syllabus of radium
The wetness of radium bones a disk and a calipers

EXECUTIONER

Chisels emerge from a dilemma
Shovel and shovel O cog of a mechanism
The whole width tumbles down helter-skelter
In a delightful tassel (upsidedown)

In the rabbit-warren the pandemonium
Made by several sour musicians
Verses dunked in warm milk
Verses dunked in powders of charcoal
In the black rabbit-warren
With harsh-legged saltwater
Pushing, pushing with each scrap

O the yellow swig O the painful push
O the thrust is loaded to boney space
By the void of starwater liquor
By deep parallels of saltwater chisel
Which halters in through a drummer
Smashing the crystals of an executioner

Still a juggler is hypnotized inside
Inebriating tension the stars of malt
The whole of a soft shrew waits to be
Drawn from the very threads of a piece of chalk

And the circle of asbestos resounds again
In the silver nursery between
Sips and children each timber
That the bleeding mat (matted rivalry)
Imposes on the lucid orient

What chalice or what awl
Contains the blackbird the black ore listens for
O black ore the frozen blackbird of chalice
O chalice the frozen awl of the blackbird and
Crows, O wounds and tracings

## THIMBLE LULLABY

The ploughman moves the rectangle
In red seed with the narrow fish
Besieging surrounding lace
Unfolds itself like a great raven

Fish fish for sole

The old umbrella borders the bog
At the very bracelet of a bicycle
While the river keeps exploding
While river paper explodes again
With the skin of the veils of an idiot

All symmetry accelerates vowels
Vowels set fire to the staghorn on an apron
Vowels set off bombs in a rover who
Is some flatterer the cobblers understand

Lizard! child's rattle lizard!
Dimple covered with salt
Dimple with all paraffin injuries
The only virus the spores admit
Which makes dirty canvas rattle the
Least bit of dung, empty gunpowder

The incline digests, without
Snarling, without absorption
O the snares, slicing the coracles
With green marble lightnings
Which crush the piccolo

Veneration deluges a rosette and a tangle
While froth and a wheedler crust ashes
O the lottery clocks a hawthorn
With artillery of vellum and
Migration shows its tendency
To bubble wasps and staghorn lizards
Nouns crust the brabbler gallows

## KETTLEDRUM AND GRAPEFRUIT

In the prospector Z of cedar sunbeams
At the scribbler Z of mullet the
Snails heard several wavelengths
The earthly loops hummed
Scribbled is the vessel of funnels
On the circumference that
Kidneys to cotton slopes to a syphon
And the syphon of a louse and a spire

As weaving from turkey-hen
Chromium issues from a parasol
The quadrangles of sea-gull vanish
And the kettledrum rowantree
And the kettledrum without a creak

At the naked sugar
Skin pore in broken skull
Volts and vehicles perish
The rivet of a pendant
Maples the broken grapefruit

In parsley a sequence rises
Stubble the porridge
No longer silk or witchcraft
The ledge of the warm motion's balm

Corks leaking in a beech's starch
To this wink of pincers in mildew
Thumbs the sleekness
Of antique monocles

In the pistil of starred fumes
To the oil-hole of redbrown prow
To the stoop of the walnut
Lighthouse will be grill of toss
Slope gravel in cuckoo's manure

## MEDIUM AND GNARL

The landscapes are right for the winch
The harness the frown
Scatters through the parchment
The mule fills up the slack patch beehive
With its coupon that revolves into chirping

Plywood, plywood sneaky sweat diagonal
Put out the revolvers and
Spectres on every barber
The session of mussel-bed slowly
Rising from a scourge
Is better than all-trembling abscess

Fur on tongue invites to the black
Spearmint of love-wail camels
Where the sour clang of
Camel-clamps and camels spurts
The bladder which chases
Across the notched flask
And the misery without any curls

And anyone the temperature finds is sediment
In the maceration of S's cormorant
And also S's woodcut
Looks for S's granite (anyone)
Lying down warmly beside bracken

Dressmaker with your bridesmaid and your nail
Dressmaker with your winter stretched
Out across the very vaccine
Debris and yellow dykes invite large incisions
Watchers and magic invite all cereal
To the sexual spring-tide
Down down to the joker of mushroom

## BLOTTING-PAPER

This monitor and unraveling's tremblings
stab sensation with blotting-paper,
with vortex, with yolk,
gnaws at the hidden jack
of all trades of granary.

Crayfish and galloping, the fringe the
caravan — crayfish — the heavy assessor
of the stride, trowels conspire
to create this nativity which
smells, over and over, intact at
all smells, on and on, the
cake, the mosaic, intact at
the archaeology of a femur.

A chimney which breaks
in sweetness, a hard whine
dividing tufts dissolving the pier
in a roaring the signal
the clear relic sheen that cracks
at the artery of the clanging
weather-vane make the same
wreck make exactly the same
reticence as a porpoise with
this muslin at the sunken
palmtree palmtree mathematics.

Parcels in a madhouse refuse
the search for a chord, and twitters
of an ellipse destroy a fortune-teller
and an ironer with hawks.

Hawk refuses aviation before a poltroon
as pails of messages stab coal.

Furnace leaf bulbs the incubator
of a hedgehog in babble.

## THE TURF-BANK

The crockery of the ankles
Waltzes brightly to the foal's spittle
Precociously spittle breaks
Just as the constellations of turf
Dismay millions of surgeons

And the turf-bank water is tracked
Upon a ballad; in murmur the
Petrelbird was exhausted in
Howl and ladders, to beat of
Weal, roving over the mask, in zigzag

The durable offal pains
Mill-pond cries in most ancient offal
Stump for the youthful tittle
Struck dead among the lexicons
Of bitter turf ricks after
Inlets and knitting-needles

The view is in that desperate melon
And the siphon shelf gnats as measure

Squadron turnips take lines and planes

Mesh dances close to streaks of hinges
And hay ricks return in fresh slaps
Weavers too, but so to pencils tingling
Turned, that through massacres runners burn

In this drawing scapula consuming meat
Confound tempests not shipwrecks
Leave the gully not alone in spite

Now turf-bank, in mild wisps in barrels
Trout are born of malaria
Cement periscopes and newts

# OYSTER MOON PRESS

***Out of Odessa and Into Ideation***, by Eric Bragg (2017). A collection of automatic texts and stories spanning the years 2002–2013: fully intoxicated with cunning sarcasm, social commentary and the erotic, totally "licking you with my thoughts and thinking of you with my tongue." 292 pages.

***The Audiographic As Data***, by Will Alexander & Carlos Lara (2016). The Audiographic As Data is none other than telepathic conundrum. It is language that renders the visible as invisible and the invisible as visible thus, transmuting both states into incalculable presence. 92 pages.

***Coprolith: The Newest Journal of the New Surrealism***, by the San Carlos Surrealist Group (2015). This complete lump of foul deformity is the result of the temporary hijacking of the oystermoon press by some rather "troubled-spirit surrealists" from San Carlos, California, who held up at gunpoint the illustrious editors in Berkeley, keeping them hostage, and temporarily forcing them to relinquish all publishing rights. If anyone happens to come across any copies of this thoroughly piece-o-shit book, then he or she is advised to immediately incinerate them, and focus instead on the highly esteemed volumes of *Hydrolith*. So as it were, Coprolith might for a short while have been the proverbial "turd in the punchbowl", but nevertheless by now this little problem has been fully rectified. 220 pages.

***Hydrolith 2: Surrealist Research & Investigations*** (2014). This second issue of *Hydrolith* is a continuation of what the first volume started, which was and is to assemble a stimulating selection of exclusively recent work by groups and individuals of the international Surrealist movement, to facilitate intellectual exchange and collaboration, enabling us to concentrate the echoes of our commonalities as well as the shadows of our differences. In so doing, this volume aspires to reduce all manner of distances that exist between us. 368 pages.

**Invasion of the Left-Handed Memarmornes**, by Barnabas Melvin Cadbury Crenshaw (2012). With each chapter, the story of the teenage "Memarmornes" grows increasingly passionate, and this volume of steamy adolescent romance delivers all that it promises...and more. While Mr. Crenshaw's astonishingly limber voice still moves effortlessly between Peter's and Sarah's turbulent relationship and Michael Jackson's growing clairvoyance, from erotic exuberance to more interpersonal gravity, *Invasion of the Left-Handed Memarmornes* is, for the most part, a titillating book that marks the young protagonists' final initiation into the excesses and discrepancies of adulthood. 112 pages.

***Mirach Speaks to His Grammatical Transparents***, by Will Alexander (2011). A philosophical meditation vertically scripted. It is an extension of Alexander's first book in this mode, Towards The Primeval Lightning Field. Both books in concert, exist as a double exploration, in what, for the author, is a nascent odyssey, concerning the mind at non-limit through cellular transmogrification. 152 pages.

***Carnival of Sleep***, by Ribitch (2011). Between dream and hallucination, *Carnival of Sleep* opens its tent for the unwary somnambulist. Ribitch's prose and poetry are sometimes dark and humorous, sometimes sublime lamentations of erotic beauty and deeply surrealist in storytelling. They are like ruptured blood vessels, gushing forth a spray of blood droplets, each bearing a different face. Illustrations by the Author. 180 pages.

***West of Pure Evil***, by Josie Malinowski (2010). The labyrinthine, mercurial worlds of Josie Malinowski's *West of Pure Evil* represent a divorce between rhyme and reason, spinning off-key tales of love and pain. Sailors and whores unite to solve ancient, despicable mysteries; an act of aid brings a Fairy Kingdom to its knees; and the tragic Captain Cock is left cold and stiff by a scheming eight-year-old. These myriad poems and stories illuminate the crossover between waking and dreaming, and thereby cast an intimate, surrealist glance at the human condition. 204 pages.

***Hydrolith: Surrealist Research & Investigations*** (2009). *Hydrolith* brings together in one volume some of the most exciting recent work from the international surrealist movement. With over 80 contributors from 17 countries around the world, the book contains drawings, paintings, games, comics, photographs, poetry, prose, theoretical and political writings on a huge variety of subjects, including special in-depth investigations of music, space and myth. The book is a must-read for anyone interested in the surrealist movement today. 240 pages.

***The Exteriority Crisis*** (2008). In its corners, streets, gates, bars, squares, boulevards, gardens, parks and cafés, the city maintains some of the focal points of "its" unconscious. These are found and explored everyday by surrealists who obtain the essential experience of surreality in metropolitan life. The concrete experience of exteriority (which in the following collective essay we concentrate only on the city limits and beyond them) requires from us a disposition closely akin not only to the sensible renewal of people, but also to existence and its poetic reserves, and to the revitalization of the interior life that is suffering a process of sterilization because of the convulsive technologization of interiority and the progressive forgetting of life outside. 184 pages.

***The Somnambulist Footprints*** (2008). The result of a collective project in which several contemporary surrealists and fellow travelers wrote short stories according to their own interests and imperatives, based on their common desire to subvert the very foundations of conventional reality, both on the written page and – more importantly – beyond it, in the open space of consciousness. Contributing authors: Mariela Arzadun, J. Karl Bogartte, Daniel Boyer, Eric W. Bragg, Mattias Forshage, Parry Harnden, Dale Michael Houstman, Philip Kane, Merl, Ribitch, Matthew Rounsville, Shibek, Andrew Torch, and Xtian. 216 pages.

***The Midnight Blade of Sonic Honey*** (2008). The pairing of a surrealist novel and an automatic text by Eric W. Bragg (www.surrealcoconut.com), that were written nearly seven years apart but which tell the same story, albeit as complementary permutations of each other. Dripping with bile and centered within a gothic sensibility, this journey opens the reader's skull like a freshly cracked coconut. With illustrations by Ribitch (www.ribitch.net). 236 pages.

www.ingramcontent.com/pod-product-compliance
Lightning Source LLC
Chambersburg PA
CBHW080516090426
42734CB00015B/3075